Ecumenical Praise

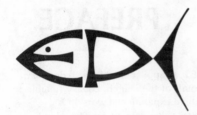

Executive Editor:
Carlton R. Young

Editorial Board:
Austin C. Lovelace
Erik Routley
Alec Wyton

Publisher:
George H. Shorney, Jr.

Contributors:
Samuel Adler
William Albright
Emma Lou Diemer
Calvin Hampton
Sr. Theophane Hytrek
Fred Kaan
Marilyn Keiser
Robert Mitchell
Daniel Moe
Lloyd Pfautsch
Carl Schalk
Heinz Werner Zimmermann

Published By:

Agape

Carol Stream, Illinois 60187

PREFACE

ECUMENICAL PRAISE is a supplemental hymnal designed to serve the growing points of the church. Equally suitable to stand alone in places where experimental worship is planned, or to supplement a denominational hymnal, it could enrich the worship of sanctuary, campus or convention by injecting into it some of the best in contemporary and classical hymnody.

Fully *catholic* in its spread of texts, tunes, poets and composers, the book encourages the use of a creative and innovative approach to the music of the church. Great care has been taken to make this a book for the worshiper prepared to contribute to, and participate in, the church's growth.

Appreciation is expressed to the distinguished contributors who were responsible for providing the broad range of materials which became the essential fabric of ECUMENICAL PRAISE. Every effort has been made to obtain proper copyright permissions and any omissions will be corrected in later editions.

THE EDITORS

Father, We Thank Thee

1

Didache, c. 110
Tr. by F. Bland Tucker

William Albright
Albright

2 Blessed Art Thou, O Lord

Adapted by Alan Luff from Luke 1:68

Eric Reid
Offertory Canticle

Bless - ed art thou, O Lord the God of Is - ra - el our Fa - ther For ev - er and for ev - er.

f Choir and Congregation (in unison)

For all things come of thee, And of thine own have we

and in the earth___ are thine. For

thine___ is the king-dom. For all things

+ Congregation

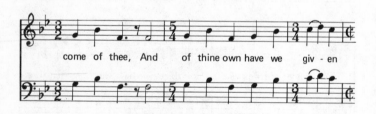

come of thee, And of thine own have we giv-en

thee. Thou art ex-al-ted as

Choir only

head a - bove all; both rich - es and hon - or

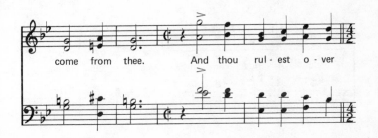

come from thee. And thou rul - est o - ver

+ Congregation

all. For all things come of thee, and

of thine own have we giv - en thee.

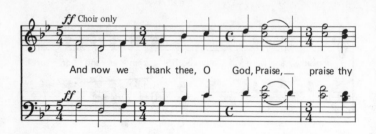

And now we thank thee, O God, Praise,___ praise thy

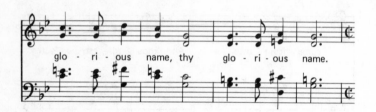

glo - ri - ous name, thy glo - ri - ous name.

+ Congregation

Bless - ed be thou, For all things

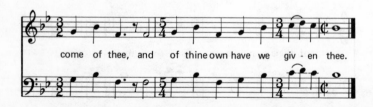

come of thee, and of thine own have we giv - en thee.

God Is Our Defense and Strength

3

Psalm 46
English Text by Marian J. Johns

Heinz Werner Zimmermann
Hymnus

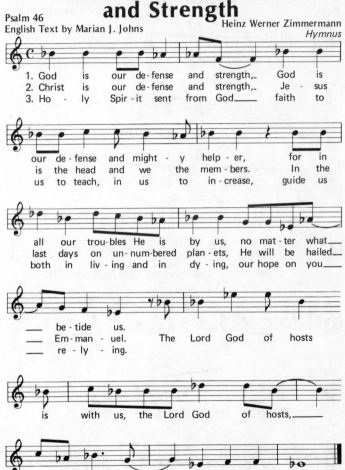

1. God is our de-fense and strength,_ God is our de-fense and might-y help-er, for in all our trou-bles He is by us, no mat-ter what_ be-tide us. The Lord God of hosts is with us, the Lord God of hosts,_ Ja-cob's God is_ our strong de-fense.

2. Christ is our de-fense and strength,_ Je - sus is the head and we the mem-bers. In the last days on un-num-bered plan-ets, He will be hailed_ Em-man-u-el.

3. Ho - ly Spir-it sent from God_ faith to us to teach, in us to in-crease, guide us both in liv-ing and in dy-ing, our hope on you_ re - ly - ing.

4

O Be Joyful in the Lord

Psalm 100

Carlton R. Young
Jubilate Deo

O be joy-ful in the Lord, all ye

lands: Serve the Lord with glad-ness, and

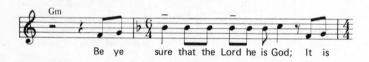

come be-fore his pres-ence with a song.

Be ye sure that the Lord he is God; It is

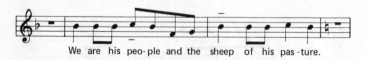

he that has made us and not___ we our-selves;

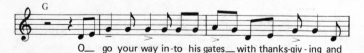

We are his peo-ple and the sheep of his pas-ture.

O___ go your way in-to his gates___ with thanks-giv-ing and

5 My Shepherd Is the Lord

Psalm 22 (23)
Grail Version

Music and Antiphon I by Joseph Gelineau
Antiphon II by A. Gregory Murray

Antiphon I

My shep-herd is the Lord, noth-ing in-deed shall I want.

Antiphon II

His good-ness shall fol-low me al-ways to the end of my days.

1. The
2. He guides me a-
3. You have pre - pared a
4. Surely goodness and
5. To the Father and

1. Lord is my shepherd; there is
2. long the right path: he is
3. banquet for me in the
4. kindness shall follow me all the
5. Son give glory, give

1. nothing I shall want.
2. true to his name. If I should
3. sight of my foes. My
4. days of my life. In the
5. glory to the Spirit. To God who

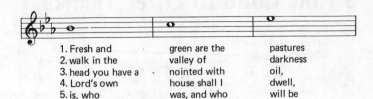

1. Fresh and   green are the   pastures
2. walk in the   valley of   darkness
3. head you have a - nointed with   oil,
4. Lord's own   house shall I   dwell,
5. is, who   was, and who   will be

1. where he   gives   me re - pose.   Near
2.   no   evil   would I   fear.   You are
3. _____
4. _____
5. _____

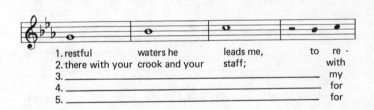

1. restful   waters he   leads me,   to re -
2. there with your crook and your   staff;   with
3. _____ my
4. _____ for
5. _____ for

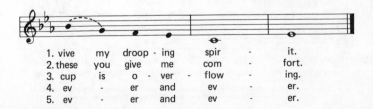

1. vive   my   droop - ing   spir - it.
2. these   you   give   me   com - fort.
3. cup   is   o - ver - flow - ing.
4. ev - er   and   ev - er.
5. ev - er   and   ev - er.

6 How Good to Offer Thanks

Psalm 92
Adapted by Emily Chisholm

Rolf Schweizer

Antiphon

How good to of - fer thanks to God, our

Fa - ther, to play in hon - or of th' Al -

might - y! How good to of - fer thanks to God, our

Fa - ther, to play in hon - or of th' Al -

Fine Verses

might - y Re-deem - er!   1. To sing your love at
                          2. You make us shout in

day - break and your mer - cy and faith-ful - ness ev' -
tri - umph and with joy cel - e-brate all your might-

- ry night, with ten stringed lute and with
- y works; your thoughts are past un - der -

D.C. al Fine

zith - er, with mer - ry harp to praise you!
stand - ing, your deeds be - yond con - ceiv - ing!

Sing O Heavens

Psalm 126

Peter Tranchell

Antiphon

Sing O heav - ens and be joy-ful O earth, and break forth in-to sing-ing, O moun-tains: For the Lord hath com-fort-ed his peo - ple and will have mer - cy up-on his af - flict - ed.

Verse

1. When the Lord turned a - gain the cap-ti - vi - ty of Si - on;
3. Then said they a-mong the hea - then:

8

Praise the Lord

Psalm 150
Adapted by Erik Routley

Barry Chevannes
Tamil

Praise the Lord!___ Praise the Lord!___ Praise the
Lord on___ earth and in the___ heav'ns: let all
things that___ breathe__ praise the___ Lord! Lord!

1. Praise the Fa-ther in his ho-ly place:
praise him in the fir-ma-ment of his power! power!

Praise the Fa-ther for his might-y works:
praise him for his ex-cel-lent great-ness. great-ness.

9

New Songs
of Celebration Render

Psalm 98
Adapted by Erik Routley

Genevan Psalter, 1551
Rendez à Dieu

1. New   songs   of   cel - e - bra - tion ren - der
2. Joy - ful - ly, heart - i - ly   re - sound - ing,
3. Riv - ers and seas and tor - rents roar - ing,

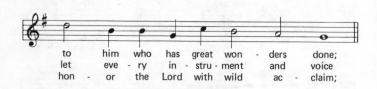

to   him who has great won - ders done;
let   eve - ry in - stru - ment and   voice
hon - or   the Lord with wild   ac - claim;

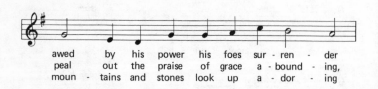

awed   by   his power his foes sur - ren - der
peal   out the praise of grace a - bound - ing,
moun - tains and stones look up   a - dor - ing

and   fall be - fore the might - y   One.
call - ing the whole world to   re - joice.
and   find a voice to praise his name.

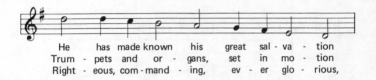

He   has made known his   great sal - va - tion
Trum - pets and or - gans, set in mo - tion
Right - eous, com-mand - ing, ev - er glo - rious,

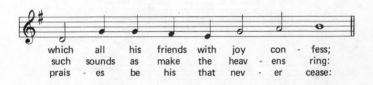

which all his friends with joy con - fess;
such sounds as make the heav - ens ring:
prais - es be his that nev - er cease:

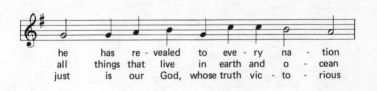

he   has re - vealed to eve - ry na - tion
all   things that live in earth and o - cean
just   is our God, whose truth vic - to - rious

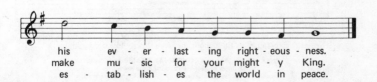

his   ev - er - last - ing right - eous - ness.
make   mu - sic for your might - y King.
es - tab - lish - es the world in peace.

10

Sing to the Lord a New Song

From Psalm 98

Samuel Adler

*Keep the clapping going throughout the piece exactly like this beginning.

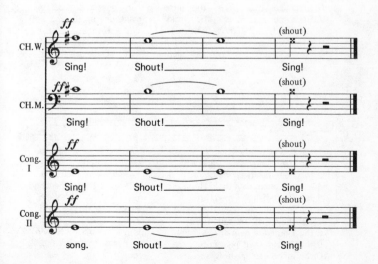

11

Remember Thy Servants, Lord

Tr. by M. M. Gowen   From the Russian Orthodox Liturgy

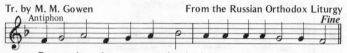

Re-mem-ber thy ser-vants, Lord, when com-eth thy glo-rious reign.

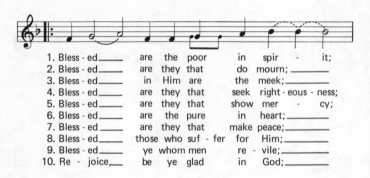

1. Bless - ed____ are the poor in spir - it;
2. Bless - ed____ are they that do mourn; ____
3. Bless - ed____ in Him are the meek;____
4. Bless - ed____ are they that seek right - eous - ness;
5. Bless - ed____ are they that show mer - cy;
6. Bless - ed____ are the pure in heart;____
7. Bless - ed____ are they that make peace;____
8. Bless - ed____ those who suf - fer for Him;____
9. Bless - ed____ ye whom men re - vile;____
10. Re - joice,____ be ye glad in God;____

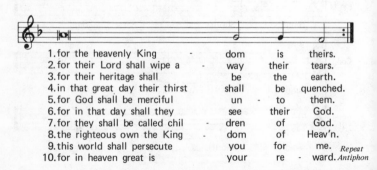

1. for the heavenly King - dom is theirs.
2. for their Lord shall wipe a - way their tears.
3. for their heritage shall be the earth.
4. in that great day their thirst shall be quenched.
5. for God shall be merciful un - to them.
6. for in that day shall they see their God.
7. for they shall be called chil - dren of God.
8. the righteous own the King - dom of Heav'n.
9. this world shall persecute you for me. *Repeat*
10. for in heaven great is your re - ward. *Antiphon*

12
Magnificat and Nunc Dimittis

Luke 1:46-55; 2:29-32

Ralph Vaughan Williams

Moderato (not too slow)

My soul doth mag-ni-fy the Lord; and my

spir-it hath re-joi-ced in God my Sav-iour. For

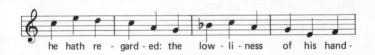

he hath re-gard-ed: the low-li-ness of his hand-

maid-en.___ For be-hold from hence-forth:

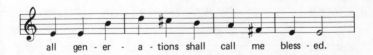

all gen-er-a-tions shall call me bless-ed.

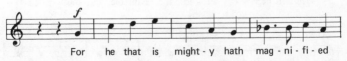

For he that is might-y hath mag-ni-fi-ed

rich he hath sent emp-ty a - way. He re - mem - b'ring his___ mer - cy hath hol - pen his ser - vant Is - ra - el: As he prom - ised to our___ fore - fa - thers, A - bra - ham and his seed for - ev - er. Glo - ry be to the Fa - ther, and to the Son; and to the Ho - ly Ghost; As it was in the be - gin - ning, is

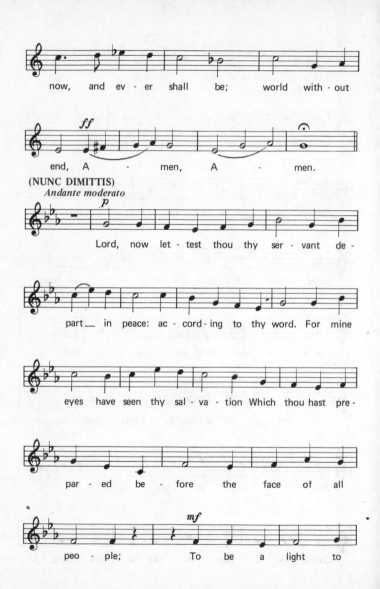

now, and ev - er shall be; world with - out

ff

end, A - men, A - men.

(NUNC DIMITTIS)
Andante moderato

p

Lord, now let - test thou thy ser - vant de -

part__ in peace: ac - cord - ing to thy word. For mine

eyes have seen thy sal - va - tion Which thou hast pre -

par - ed be - fore the face of all

mf

peo - ple; To be a light to

13 This Is the Feast

Lutheran Communion Service Number Two

Daniel Moe
Feast of Victory

(to Refrain)

join in the hymn of all cre - a - tion.

Verse 4

Bless - ing, hon - or, glo - ry and

might be to God and the Lamb for - ev - er.

A - men.

Refrain (after Verse 4)

This is the feast of

vic - to - ry for our God, for the Lamb___ who was

slain has be - gun his reign. Al - le -

lu - ia, Al - le - lu - ia, Al - le - lu - ia.

14 Jesus Christ Has Come into Capernaum

Juhani Forsberg
Tr. by Emily Chisholm

Juhani Forsberg
Capernaum

1. Je - sus Christ has come in - to Ca -
2. In the o - ver - crowd - ed house the
3. As he lies be - fore his feet, the
4. Je - sus puts a ques - tion now, and
5. And the man stands up and walks, al -

1. per - na - um, his cit - y, some there are who
2. Lord speaks to the peo - ple. Look, they're bring - ing
3. Lord looks at the suf - ferer, speaks a word of
4. asks them for an an - swer: Solo III 'Tell me, an - y -
5. though his knees are shak - ing. All can see that

1. praise him, but the oth - ers shout in pro - test.
2. in the par - a - ly - tic on a stretch - er.
3. power to him, and man - y are of - fend - ed:
4. bod - y, which is eas - i - er to man - age.
5. he can walk. They lis - ten to his prais - es.

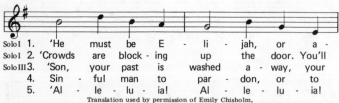

Solo I 1. 'He must be E - li - jah, or a -
Solo I 2. 'Crowds are block - ing up the door. You'll
Solo III 3. 'Son, your past is washed a - way, your
4. Sin - ful man to par - don, or to
5. 'Al - le - lu - ia! Al - le - lu - ia!

15 And There Will Be Signs

Luke 21:25-28

Stephen Chatman
Hymn

bod - ing of what is com - ing on the world; for the

pow - ers of the hea - vens will be sha - ken.

And then they will see the Son of Man

com - ing in a cloud with pow - er___ and great

glo - ry. Look up and raise your

heads, be - cause your re - demp - tion is

draw - ing near.___

16 Come, Holy Ghost, Our Souls Inspire

Attr. to Rabanus Maurus
Tr. by John Cosin

Vesperale Romanum Mechlin, 1848
Veni Creator Spiritus

1. Come, Ho-ly Ghost, our souls in-spire,
3. Thy bless-ed unc-tion from a-bove
5. A-noint and cheer our soil-ed face
7. Teach us to know the Fa-ther, Son,

And light-en with ce-les-tial fire.
Is com-fort, life, and fire of love.
With the a-bun-dance of thy grace.
And thee, of both, to be but One,

2. Thou the a-noint-ing Spir-it art,
4. En-a-ble with per-pet-ual light
6. Keep far our foes, give peace at home:
8. That through the a-ges all a-long,

D.C.

Who dost thy sev'n-fold gifts im-part.
The dull-ness of our blind-ed sight.
Where thou art guide, no ill can come.
This may be our end-less song:

9. Praise to thy e-ter-nal mer-it,

Fa-ther, Son and Ho-ly Spir-it. A-men.

On This Day Earth Shall Ring

Piae Cantiones
Tr. by Jane M. Joseph

Personent Hodie
Arr. by Gustav T. Holst

1. On this day earth shall ring
2. His the doom, ours the mirth;
3. God's bright star, o'er his head,
4. On this day an - gels sing;

With the song chil - dren sing To the Lord,
When he came down to earth Beth - le - hem
Wise Men three to him led; Kneel they low
With their song earth shall ring, Prais - ing Christ,

Christ our King, Born on earth to save us;
saw his birth; Ox and ass be - side him
by his bed, Lay their gifts be - fore him,
heav - en's King, Born on earth to save us;

Refrain

Him the Fa - ther gave us.
From the cold would hide him.
Praise him and a - dore him.   Id - e - o - o - o,
Peace and love he gave us.

Id - e - o - o - o, Id - e - o

glo - ri - a in ex - cel - sis De - o!

18 You We Praise as God

Attr. to Niceta, Bishop of Ramesiana, 4th Century

Tr. by Alan Luff

Erik Routley
Te Deum

Antiphon I *Allegro (o = o of verses)*

Ex - tol the Lord your God, for the
Lord____ your____ God is ho - ly.

Verses 1-5

1. You we praise as God; you we ac -
2. To you all orders of being, ev' - ry
3. Ho - ly, Ho - ly, Ho - ly, Captain of the
4. The shin - ing dance of your messengers, your pro - phets'
5. Pro - claim their faith in you, Father of

1. claim as Lord; you the whole earth worships,
2. pow'r that is, those who wait closest up - on you
3. heav'n - ly armies, all time and space, and be-yond
4. song of praise, the white-robed army who died for you,
5. might un - bounded, Son, a - lone to be worshipped,

1. e - ternal Fa - ther of all. *(Antiphon I)*
2. raise their end - less____ cry: *(Verse 3)*
3. re - flect your king - ly____ glory! *(Antiphon I)*
4. the Church through-out the ____ world. *(Verse 5)*
5. Spirit, sent to our aid. *(Antiphon II)*

Antiphon II

Who is the King of Glo-ry?___ The Lord of Hosts, he is the King of Glo-ry!

Verses 6-8

6. You, Christ, are the King of Glory,
7. By de-stroying the sting of death
8. Bought at the price of your life

you are the Father's e-ternal Son.
you gave be-lievers a road to God's presence,
we your household pray for your help:

When to save the world you became man,
where you sit en-throned in light;
Give us the fullness of life

you did not shrink from a hu-man birth. *(Antiphon II)*
we a-wait your coming as Judge. *(Verse 8)*
for-ever with all who are yours. *(Antiphon II)*

After the last Antiphon

Al-le-lu-ia, Al-le-lu-ia!

19

Come, Thou Holy Spirit

Latin, 12th Century
Tr. by Edward Caswall

Iain Hamilton
Golden Sequence

Slowly (♩ = 72)

1. Come, Thou Ho - ly Spir - it come!____
2. Thou, of com - for - ters the best;____
3. O most bless - ed Light____ di - vine,____
4. Heal our wounds, our strength____ re - new;____
5. On the faith - ful, who____ a - dore____

1. And from Thy ce - les - tial home____
2. Thou, the soul's most wel - come guest;____
3. Shine with - in these hearts of Thine,____
4. On our dry - ness pour Thy dew;____
5. And con - fess Thee, ev - er - more____

1. Shed a ray of light____ di - vine!____
2. Sweet re - fresh - ment here____ be - low;____
3. And our in - most be - ing fill!____
4. Wash the stains of guilt____ a - way:____
5. In Thy sev'n - fold gift____ de - scend;____

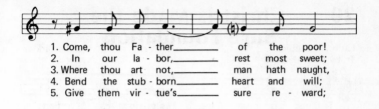

1. Come, thou Fa - ther _____ of the poor!
2. In our la - bor, _____ rest most sweet;
3. Where thou art not, _____ man hath naught,
4. Bend the stub - born _____ heart and will;
5. Give them vir - tue's _____ sure re - ward;

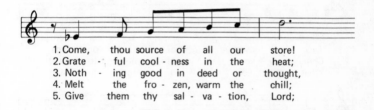

1. Come, thou source of all our store!
2. Grate - ful cool - ness in the heat;
3. Noth - ing good in deed or thought,
4. Melt the fro - zen, warm the chill;
5. Give them thy sal - va - tion, Lord;

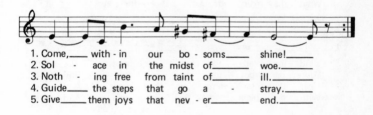

1. Come, _____ with - in our bo - soms _____ shine! _____
2. Sol - ace in the midst of _____ woe. _____
3. Noth - ing free from taint of _____ ill. _____
4. Guide _____ the steps that go a - stray. _____
5. Give _____ them joys that nev - er _____ end. _____

After last stanza

A - men. _____ A - men. _____

20 Christ Is Made the Sure Foundation

Latin 7th Century
Tr. by John M. Neale

Richard Dirksen
Christ Church

mf With majesty

1. Christ is made the sure foun - da - tion,
2. All that ded - i - ca - ted cit - y,
3. To this tem - ple, where we call thee,
4. Here vouch - safe to all thy ser - vants

Christ the head and cor - ner - stone,
Dear - ly loved of God on high,
Come, O Lord of hosts to - day;
What they ask of thee to gain;

Cho - sen of the Lord, and pre - cious,
In ex - ult - ant ju - bi - la - tion
With thy won - ted lov - ing - kind - ness
What they gain from thee for - ev - er

Bind - ing all the church in one; Ho - ly
Pours per - pet - ual mel - o - dy; God the
Hear thy ser - vants as they pray, And thy
With the bless - ed to re - tain, And here -

f

Si - on's help for - ev - er, And her
One in Three a - dor - ing In glad
full - est ben - e - dic - tion Shed with -
aft - er in thy glo - ry Ev - er -

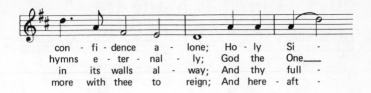

con - fi - dence a - lone; Ho - ly Si -
hymns e - ter - nal - ly; God the One___
in its walls al - way; And thy full -
more with thee to reign; And here - aft -

on's help for - ev - er, And her
in Three a - dor - ing In glad
est ben - e - dic - tion Shed with -
er in thy glo - ry Ev - er -

con - fi - dence a - lone.
hymns___ e - ter - nal - ly.
in___ its walls al - way.
more___ with thee to reign. A - men.

Descant (Stanza 4)

Here vouch - safe to all___ thy ser - vants

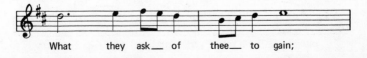

What they ask___ of thee___ to gain;

What they gain from thee____ for - ev - er

With the bless - ed to re - tain,____ And here -

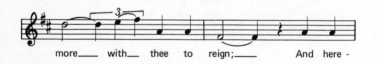

aft - er in__ thy glo - ry Ev - er -

more____ with__ thee to reign;____ And here -

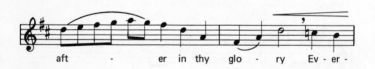

aft - er in thy glo - ry Ev - er -

more____ with thee__ to reign. A - men.

All People That on Earth 21
Do Dwell

William Kethe

Old 100th
Arr. by Benjamin Britten

All peo - ple that on earth do dwell, Sing

to the Lord with cheer - ful voice! Him serve with fear, His

praise forth tell, Come ye be - fore Him and re - joice.

Soprano

O en - ter_ then His gates with_ praise, Ap -

Alto

O en - ter then His gates with praise, Ap -

Choir and Congregation

O en - ter then His gates with praise, Ap -

proach with joy His courts___ un - to, Praise,

proach with_joy His courts un - to, Praise,

proach with joy His courts un - to, Praise,

laud and bless His name___ al - ways, For

laud and bless His name___ al - ways, For

laud and bless His name al - ways, For

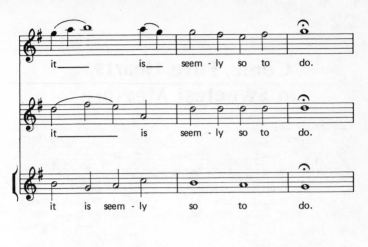

it____ is____ seem - ly so to do.

it_____ is seem - ly so to do.

it is seem - ly so to do.

For why? the Lord our God is good:

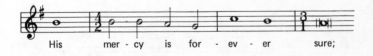

His mer - cy is for - ev - er sure;

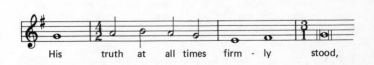

His truth at all times firm - ly stood,

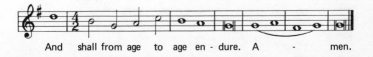

And shall from age to age en - dure. A - men.

22

Come, Pure Hearts,
in Sweetest Measure

12th Century Latin
Tr. by R. Campbell

Ned Rorem
Pure Hearts

1. Come,___ pure hearts,___ in___ sweet - est
2. See___ the riv - ers___ four___ that
3. O___ that we,___ thy___ truth___ con -

meas - ure Sing___ of___ those___ who___
glad - den, With___ their___ streams,___ the___
fess - ing, And___ thy___ ho - ly___

spread___ the___ treas - ure In___ the
bet - ter___ E - den Plant - ed
word___ pos - sess - ing, Je - sus

ho - ly gos - pels shrined; Bless - ed
by___ our Lord___ most dear; Christ___ the
may___ thy love___ a - dore; Un - to

ti - dings   of___ sal - va - tion,
foun - tain,   these___ the   wa - ters;
thee___ our   voic - es   rais - ing,

Peace   on___ earth___ their   proc - la -
Drink,   O___ Si -   on's   sons   and___
Thee   with___ all___   thy   ran - somed___

ma - tion,   Love   from___ God   to
daugh - ters,   Drink,   and___ find   sal -
prais - ing,   Ev - er___   and   for -

1., 2.   **3.**

lost   man - kind.
va - tion   here.
ev - er -   more.   A - men.___

23 I Bind unto Myself Today

St. Patrick's Breastplate
Tr. by C. F. Alexander

Traditional Irish Melodies
St. Patrick and *Deirdre*
Arr. by C. V. Stanford

1. I bind un - to__ my - self__ to -
2. I bind this day__ to me__ for -
3. I bind un - to__ my - self__ the__
4. I bind un - to__ my - self__ to -
5. I bind un - to__ my - self__ to -

1. day__ The strong__ Name of__ the
2. ev - er, By power__ of faith,__ Christ's
3. power__ Of the__ great love__ of
4. day__ The vir - tues of__ the
5. day__ The power__ of God__ to

1. Trin - i - ty,__ By in - vo - ca - tion
2. In - car - na-tion; His bap - tism__ in__ the
3. cher - u - bim;__ The sweet__ "Well__ done"__ in
4. star - lit heav'n,__ The glo - rious__ sun's__ life -
5. hold and lead,__ His eye__ to__ watch,_ his

1. of the same,__ The__ Three in__ One,__
2. Jor - dan riv - er; His__ death on__ cross__
3. judg - ment hour;__ The__ ser - vice__ of__
4. giv - ing ray,__ The__ white - ness__ of__
5. might to stay,__ His__ ear to__ heark -

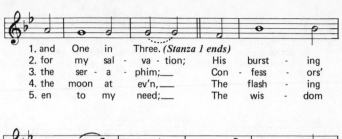

1. and One in Three. *(Stanza 1 ends)*
2. for my sal - va - tion; His burst - ing
3. the ser - a - phim;__ Con - fess - ors'
4. the moon at ev'n, __ The flash - ing
5. en to my need;__ The wis - dom

2. from the__ spi - ced tomb; His ri - ding
3. faith, a - pos - tles' word, The pa - tri - archs'
4. of the__ light - ning free, The whirl - ing
5. of my__ God to teach, His hand to

2. up_____ the heav'n - ly way; His
3. prayers,__ the pro - phets' scrolls; All
4. wind's__ tem - pest - uous shocks, The
5. guide,__ his shield to ward; The

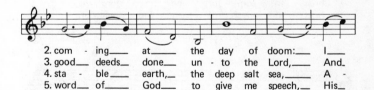

2. com - ing__ at__ the day of doom:__ I__
3. good__ deeds__ done__ un - to the Lord,__ And__
4. sta - ble__ earth,__ the deep salt sea,__ A -
5. word__ of__ God__ to give me speech,__ His__

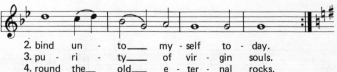

2. bind un - to__ my - self to - day.
3. pu - ri - ty__ of vir - gin souls.
4. round the__ old__ e - ter - nal rocks.
5. heav'n - ly__ host__ to be my guard.

6. Christ be with me, Christ with - in me,
   Christ be - neath me, Christ a - bove me,

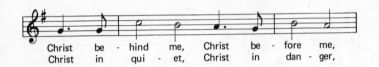

Christ be - hind me, Christ be - fore me,
Christ in qui - et, Christ in dan - ger,

Christ be - side me, Christ to win me,
Christ in hearts of all that love me,

Christ to com - fort and re - store me,
Christ in mouth of friend and strang - er.

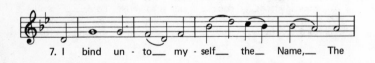

7. I bind un - to__ my - self__ the__ Name,__ The

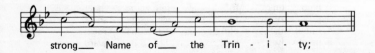

strong__ Name of__ the Trin - i - ty;

24

When Christ Was Born
of Mary Free

Anonymous, 15th Century

John Gardner
Wildersmouth

With bounce (♩ = 64)

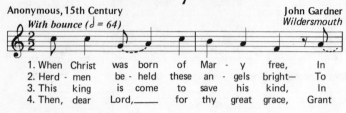

1. When Christ was born of Mar—y free, In
2. Herd-men be-held these an-gels bright— To
3. This king is come to save his kind, In
4. Then, dear Lord,___ for thy great grace, Grant

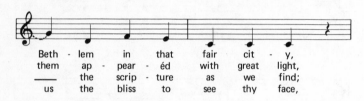

Beth— lem in that fair cit—y,
them ap— pear—éd with great light,
___ the scrip-ture as we find;
us the bliss to see thy face,

An— gels sung___ e'er with mirth and glee,___
And said, 'God's___ Son is born this night':___
There— fore this___ song have we in mind:___
Where we may___ sing to thy so— lace.___

High Voices

In ex— cel— sis glo— ri— a,

Low Voices

In ex— cel— sis glo— ri— a,

glo - ri - a, glo - ri - a,

glo - ri - a, glo - ri -

in ex - cel - sis glo - ri - a,_____ Chris -

a, in ex - cel - sis glo - ri - a,_____

to pa - re - mus can - ti - ca, In

Chris - to pa - re - mus can - ti - ca,_____

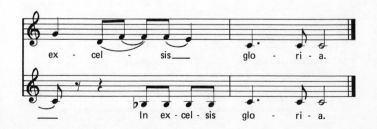

ex - cel - sis_____ glo - ri - a.

_____ In ex - cel - sis glo - ri - a.

25

A Mighty Fortress Is Our God

Martin Luther
Tr. by F. Samuel Janzow

Martin Luther
Ein' Feste Burg

1. A might - y For - tress is_____ our God
2. To trust in our vain hu - man might
3. Though de - mons' roar - ing fills_____ the world
4. That Word, de - spite all foes,_____ will stand,

Strong Shield and stur - dy Wea - pon,
Would forge our quick sur - ren - der.
In - tent on our dam - na - tion,
And let them al - ways hear_____ it!

Rock of de - fense and smit - ing Rod
One Man wrings vic - tory from_____ the fight,
We scorn our fear and raise_____ un - furled
The Word stands by us, His_____ strong hand

When hordes of e - vil threat - en.
By God's choice our De - fend - er.
The ban - ner of sal - va - tion.
Sup - plies His gifts and Spir - it.

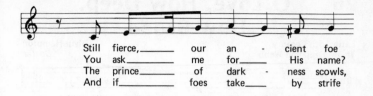

Still fierce,_____ our an - cient foe
You ask_____ me for_____ His name?
The prince_____ of dark - ness scowls,
And if_____ foes take____ by strife

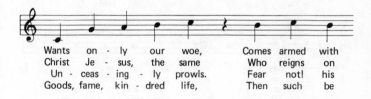

Wants on - ly our woe, Comes armed with
Christ Je - sus, the same Who reigns on
Un - ceas - ing - ly prowls. Fear not! his
Goods, fame, kin - dred life, Then such be

brute might, De - ceit and dead - ly spite.
God's throne, Lord Sa - ba - oth a - lone,
doom's sealed, For God Him - self re - vealed
our loss, For we still keep the cross,

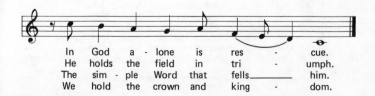

In God a - lone is res - cue.
He holds the field in tri - umph.
The sim - ple Word that fells_____ him.
We hold the crown and king - dom.

26   O Love, How Deep, How Broad

Latin 15th Century
Tr. by Benjamin Webb

Calvin Hampton
De Tar

1. O love, how deep, how broad, how high,
2. For us bap - tized, for us He bore
3. For us He prayed, for us He taught,
4. For us to wick - ed men be - trayed,
5. For us He rose from death a - gain,
6. All glo - ry to our Lord and God

1. How pass - ing thought and fan - ta - sy,
2. His ho - ly fast, and hun - ger'd sore;
3. For us His dai - ly works He wrought,
4. Scourged, mocked, in pur - ple robe ar - rayed,
5. For us He went on high to reign;
6. For love so deep, so high, so broad;

1. That God, the Son of God, should take
2. For us temp - ta - tions sharp He knew;
3. By words and signs and ac - tions, thus
4. He bore the shame - ful cross and death;
5. For us He sent His Spir - it here
6. The Trin - i - ty whom we a - dore

1. Our mor - tal form for mor - tals' sake.
2. For us the temp - ter o - ver - threw.
3. Still seek - ing not Him - self, but us.
4. For us gave up His dy - ing breath.
5. To guide, to strength - en, and to cheer.
6. For ev - er and for ev - er - more. A - men.

O Jesus Christ,
Our Lord Most Dear

Heinrich von Laufenburg
Tr. by Catherine Winkworth

Richard Dirksen
Angus

1. O Je-sus Christ, our Lord most dear, As Thou wast once an in-fant here, So give this child of Thine, we pray, Thy grace and bless-ing day by day. O ho-ly Jesus, Lord di-vine, we pray Thee guard this child of Thine. A - men.

2. As in Thy heav'n-ly king-dom, Lord, Thy mes-sen-gers o-bey Thy word, Send forth the suc-cor of Thy might To shield this child both day and night.

3. And all her life, let an-gels keep Her safe from harm, a-wake, a-sleep; May she not bear the cross in vain, But with Thy saints a crown at-tain.

28

Where Is This
Stupendous Stranger

Christopher Smart

Alec Wyton
Kit Smart

1. Where is this stu - pen - dous strang - er?
2. O most might - y, O most ho - ly,
3. O the mag - ni - tude of meek - ness!
4. God all - bount - eous, all - cre - a - tive,

Proph - ets, shep - herds, kings, ad - vise,
Far be - yond the ser - aph's thought
Worth from worth im - mor - tal sprung,
Whom no ills from good dis - suade,

Lead me to my Mas - ter's man - ger,
Art thou then so mean and low - ly
O the strength of in - fant weak - ness,
Is in - car - nate and a na - tive

Show me where my Sav - ior lies.
As un - heed - ed proph - ets taught?
If e - ter - nal is so young!
Of the ver - y world he made.

Eternal Beam of Light Divine

Charles Wesley

Nathaniel Gawthorn
Eltham

1. E - ter - nal beam of light di -
2. Je - sus, the wea - ry wan - d'rer's
3. Thank - ful I take the cup from
4. Be thou, O Rock of A - ges,
5. Speak to my war - ring pas - sions
6. O death, where is thy sting? Where

1. vine, Foun - tain of un - ex - haust - ed
2. rest, Give me thy eas - y yoke to
3. Thee, Pre - pared and min - gled by Thy
4. nigh! So shall each mur - muring thought be
5. 'Peace!' Say to my trem - bling heart, 'Be
6. now Thy boast - ed vic - to - ry,

1. love, In whom the Fa - ther's glo - ries
2. bear, With stead - fast pa - tience arm my
3. skill, Tho' bit - ter to the taste it
4. gone, And grief and fear and care shall
5. still!' Thy pow'r my strength and for - tress
6. grave? Who shall con - tend with God? or

1. shine Thro' earth be - neath and heav'n a - bove.
2. breast With spot - less love and low - ly fear.
3. be, Pow'r - ful the wound - ed soul to heal.
4. fly, As clouds be - fore the mid - day sun.
5. is, For all things serve thy sov - 'reign will.
6. who Can hurt whom God de - lights to save?

30

Come, O Thou Traveler

Charles Wesley

Erik Routley
Woodbury

1. Come, O thou trav-el-er un-known Whom still I hold but can-not see; My com-pa-ny be-fore is gone, And I am left a-lone with Thee; With Thee all night I mean to stay And wres-tle till the break of day.___

2. I need not tell Thee who I am, My mis-er-y and sin de-clare; Thy-self hast called me by my name, Look on Thy hands and read it there. But who, I ask Thee, who art Thou? Tell me Thy name and tell me now.___

3. Yield to me now, for I am weak, But con-fi-dent in self-de-spair; Speak to my heart, in bless-ings speak; Be con-quered by my in-stant prayer. Speak or Thou nev-er hence shalt move, And tell me if Thy name is Love.___

4. 'Tis Love! 'tis Love, Thou diedst for me; I hear Thy whis-per in my heart; The morn-ing breaks, the shad-ows flee, Pure u-ni-ver-sal Love Thou art! To me, to all, Thy mer-cies move; Thy na-ture and Thy name is Love._

WRESTLING JACOB from ETERNAL LIGHT by Erik Routley.

Open, Lord, My Inward Ear
³¹

Charles Wesley

Malcolm Williamson
Obedience

1. O - pen, Lord, my in - ward ear and bid my heart re - joice; Bid my qui - et spir - it hear Thy com - fort - a - ble voice; Nev - er in the whirl - wind found, or where the earth - quake rocks the place; Still and si - lent is the sound, the whis - per of Thy grace.

2. Show me, as my soul can bear, the depth of in - bred sin; All my un - be - lief de - clare the pride that lurks with - in: Take me, whom Thy - self hast bought, and bring in - to cap - tiv - i - ty Eve - ry high as - pir - ing thought that would not stoop to Thee.

3. Lord, my time is in Thy hand, my soul to Thee con - vert; Thou canst make me un - der - stand, though I am slow of heart; Thine in whom I live and move, Thine, Lord, the work, the praise is Thine! Thou art wis - dom, pow'r, and love, and all Thou art is mine.

32 Rejoice, the Lord Is King

Charles Wesley

George F. Handel
Gopsal
Arr. by John Wilson

1. Re - joice, the Lord is King! Your
2. Je - sus the Sav - iour reigns, The
3. His king - dom can - not fail, He
4. Re - joice in glor - ious hope; Je -

Lord and King a - dore; Mor - tals, give thanks and
God of truth and love; When He had purged our
rules o'er earth and heaven; The keys of death and
sus the Judge shall come, And take His ser - vants

sing, And tri - umph ev - er - more:
stains, He took His seat a - bove:
hell Are to our Je - sus given:
up To their e - ter - nal home:

1-3.
Lift up your heart, lift up your voice; Re - joice; a -

4.
gain I say, re - joice. We soon shall hear th'arch-an-gel's voice;

The trump of God shall sound, re - joice!

Ye Servants of God

Charles Wesley

David S. Goodall
New Saraband

1. Ye serv-ants of God,— your Mas-ter pro-claim,— And pub-lish a-broad— His won-der-ful Name;— The Name all-vic-to-rious— of Je-sus ex-tol;— His King-dom is glo-rious, and rules— o-ver all.—

2. God rul-eth on high,— al-might-y to save;— And still He is nigh,— His pres-ence we have;— The great con-gre-ga-tion— His tri-umph shall sing,— As-crib-ing sal-va-tion to Je-sus our King.—

3. Sal-va-tion to God,— who sits on the throne! Let all cry a-loud,— and hon-or the Son:— The prais-es of Je-sus— the an-gels pro-claim,— Fall down on their fac-es and wor-ship the Lamb.—

4. Then let us a-dore,— and give Him His right,— All glo-ry and power, all wis-dom and might,— All hon-or and bless-ing,— with an-gels a-bove,— And thanks nev-er ceas-ing, and in-fi-nite love.—

34 Christ, Whose Glory Fills the Skies

Charles Wesley   Malcolm Williamson

1. Christ, whose glo - ry fills the skies,
Christ, the true, the on - ly Light,
Sun of Right - eous - ness, a - rise,
Tri - umph o'er the shades of night;
Day - spring from on high, be near;
Day - star, in my heart ap - pear.____

2. Dark and cheer - less is the morn
Un - ac - com - pa - nied by Thee;
Joy - less is the day's re - turn,
Till Thy mer - cy's beams I see;
Till they in - ward light im - part,
Glad my eyes, and warm my heart.____

3. Vis - it then this soul of mine,
Pierce the gloom of sin and grief;
Fill me, Ra - dian - cy Di - vine,
Scat - ter all my un - be - lief;
More and more Thy - self dis - play,
Shin - ing to the per - fect day.____

How Wondrous Great

Isaac Watts
St. 3 alt. by Caryl Micklem

Alec Wyton
Shorney

1. How won - drous great, how glo - rious
2. Our soar - ing spir - its up - ward
3. Our rea - son stretch - es all its
4. While all the heaven - ly powers con -

bright must our Cre - a - tor be, Who
rise to - wards the burn - ing throne. Fain
wings, and climbs a - bove the skies; But
spire e - ter - nal praise to sing; Let

dwells a - midst the dazz - ling light of
would we see the bless - ed Three and
still how far be - neath Thy feet our
faith in hum - ble notes a - dore the

vast e - ter - ni - ty.
the al - might - y One.
ground - ling know - ledge lies!
great mys - te - rious King.

36 Joy to the World

Isaac Watts

Emma Lou Diemer

1. Joy to the world! the Lord is come;__ Let
2. Joy to the world! the Sav - ior reigns;__ Let
3. No more let sins and sor - rows grow,__ Nor
4. He rules the world with truth and grace,__ And

earth re - ceive__ her King; Let ev - ery heart__ pre -
men their songs__ em - ploy, While fields and floods, rocks,
thorns in - fest__ the ground; He comes to make__ His
makes the na - tions prove The glo - ries of__ His

pare Him room,__ And heav - en and na - ture sing,
hills and plains__ Re - peat__ the sound - ing joy,
bless - ings flow__ Far as__ the curse is found,
right - eous - ness,__ And won - ders of His love,

And heav - en and na - ture sing, And
Re - peat__ the sound - ing joy, Re -
Far as__ the curse__ is found, Far
And won - ders of__ His love, And

heav - en and na - ture__ sing.__
peat__ the sound - ing__ joy.__
as__ the curse__ is__ found.__
won - ders of__ His love.__

1, 2, 3.   4.

My Dear Redeemer

Isaac Watts

Malcolm Williamson
Life of Christ

1. My dear Re - deem - er and my Lord, I read my du - ty in Thy Word; But in my life the law ap - pears drawn out in liv - ing char - ac - ters.
2. Such was Thy truth and such Thy zeal, such de - ference to Thy Fa - ther's will, Such love, and meek - ness so di - vine, I would trans - cribe and make them mine.
3. Cold moun - tains and the mid - night air wit - nessed the fer - vor of Thy prayer; The des - ert Thy temp - ta - tions knew, Thy con - flict and Thy vic - tory too.
4. Be Thou my pat - tern, make me bear more of Thy gra - cious im - age here; Then God, the Judge, shall own my name a - mongst the fol - lowers of the Lamb.

I read my du - ty in Thy Word, My dear Re - deem - er and my Lord.

38

Nature with Open Volume Stands

Isaac Watts

Erik Routley
Maple Grove

1. Na - ture with o - pen vol - ume stands
2. But in the grace that res - cued man,
3. Here His whole name ap - pears com - plete;
4. O the sweet won - ders of that cross
5. I would for - ev - er speak His name

1. to spread her Mak - er's praise a - broad;
2. His bright - est form of glo - ry shines;
3. nor wit can guess, nor rea - son prove,
4. where Christ my Sav - ior loved and died!
5. in sounds to mor - tal ears un - known,

1. And ev' - ry la - bor of His hands
2. Here, on the cross, 'tis fair - est drawn
3. Which of the let - ters best is writ,
4. Her no - blest life my spir - it draws
5. With an - gels join to praise the Lamb

1-4.   5.

1. shows some - thing wor - thy of a God.
2. in pre - cious blood and crim - son lines.
3. the power, the wis - dom, or the love.
4. from His dear wounds and bleed - ing side.
5. and wor - ship at His Fa - ther's throne!

Nature with Open Volume Stands

Isaac Watts

Nathaniel Gawthorn
Eltham

1. Na - ture with o - pen vol - ume stands to spread her Mak - er's praise a - broad; And ev' - ry la - bor of His hands shows some - thing wor - thy of a God.
2. But in the grace that res - cued man, His bright - est form of glo - ry shines; Here, on the cross, 'tis fair - est drawn in pre - cious blood and crim - son lines.
3. Here His whole name ap - pears com - plete; nor wit can guess, nor rea - son prove, Which of the let - ters best is writ, the power, the wis - dom, or the love.
4. O the sweet won - ders of that cross where Christ my Sav - ior loved and died! Her no - blest life my spir - it draws from His dear wounds and bleed - ing side.
5. I would for - ev - er speak His name in sounds to mor - tal ears un - known, With an - gels join to praise the Lamb and wor - ship at His Fa - ther's throne!

40 From All that Dwell
and
Praise God From Whom
All Blessings Flow

Isaac Watts
Thomas Ken

Calvin Hampton
Wyton

From all that
Praise God, from

dwell be - low__ the skies,
whom all bless - ings flow;

Let the Cre -
Praise Him, all

a - tor's praise a - rise;
crea - tures here be - low;

Let the Re -
Praise Him a -

deem - er's name__ be sung,
bove, ye heav - enly host;

Through ev - ery
Praise Fa - ther,

land by ev - ery tongue.
Son, and Ho - ly Ghost.

A - men.

God Moves in a Mysterious Way

William Cowper

London New
Arr. by Benjamin Britten

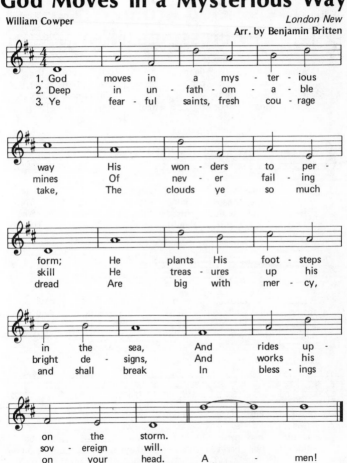

1. God moves in a mys - ter - ious way His won - ders to per - form; He plants His foot - steps in the sea, And rides up - on the storm.
2. Deep in un - fath - om - a - ble mines Of nev - er - fail - ing skill He treas - ures up his bright de - signs, And works his sov - ereign will.
3. Ye fear - ful saints, fresh cou - rage take, The clouds ye so much dread Are big with mer - cy, and shall break In bless - ings on your head. A - men!

42

Sometimes a Light Surprises

William Cowper

Jane M. Marshall
Surprise

1. Some-times a light sur-pris-es The Chris-tian while he sings; It is the Lord, who ris-es With heal-ing in his wings. When
2. In ho-ly con-tem-pla-tion We sweet-ly then pur-sue The theme of God's sal-va-tion, And find it ev-er new; Set
3. It can bring with it noth-ing But he will bear us through; Who gives the lil-ies cloth-ing Will clothe his peo-ple, too; Be-
4. Though vine nor fig tree nei-ther Their wont-ed fruit should bear, Though all the field should with-er, Nor flocks nor herds be there; Yet

43

O, Sabbath Rest of Galilee

John Greenleaf Whittier

Charles E. Ives
Serenity

*Very slowly, quietly, and sustained,
with little or no change in tempo
or volume throughout.*

O, Sab-bath rest of Gal - i - lee!_ O,
calm of hills a - bove,_____ Where Je - sus knelt to
share with_ thee_____ The si - lence_____
_ of e - ter - ni - ty_ In - ter - pret - ed by
love._____ Drop thy still dews of

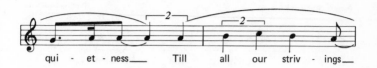

qui - et - ness___ Till all our striv - ings___

___ cease;___ Take from our souls the

strain and stress,___ And let our or - dered

lives con - fess The beau - ty of thy

peace.___

44

Rise an' Shine

Negro Spiritual

Negro Spiritual
Arr. by Edward Boatner

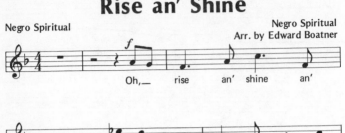

Oh,— rise an' shine an'

give God the glo-ry, glo-ry, Rise an' shine an'

give God the glo-ry, glo-ry, Rise an' shine an'

give God the glo-ry, glo-ry in the year of

Ju-bi-lee. We are— climb-ing—

Ja-cob's— lad-der, lad-der, we are— climb-ing—

Ja - cob's___ lad - der, lad - der, we are climb - ing

Ja - cob's___ lad - der, lad - der in the year of

Ju - bi - lee. Ev - 'ry___ round goes___

high - er, high - er, high - er, Ev - 'ry round goes

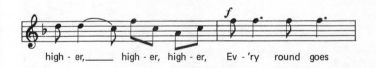

high - er,___ high - er, high - er, Ev - 'ry round goes

high - er,___ high - er, high - er, in the year of Ju - bi - lee.

Oh,— rise an' shine an' give God the glo - ry, glo - ry,

Rise an' shine an' give God the glo - ry, glo - ry,

Rise an' shine an' give God the glo - ry, glo - ry

in the year of Ju - bi - lee.— Oh,—

rise an' shine an' give God the glo - ry, glo - ry,

Rise an' shine an' give God the glo - ry, glo - ry,

Rise an' shine an' give God the glo - ry, glo - ry,

in the year of Ju - bi - lee.—

'Tis the Gift to Be Simple 45

Shaker Song

Simple Gifts
Adapted by Aaron Copland

'Tis the gift to be sim - ple, 'tis the gift to be free, 'Tis the gift to come down where you ought to be, And when we find our - selves in the place just right, 'Twill be in the val - ley of love and de - light.___ When true sim - pli - ci - ty is gained, To bow and to bend we shan't be a-shamed, To turn, turn will be our de - light 'Till by turn - ing, turn - ing we come round right.___

'Tis the

2nd time to Coda

Coda

46
What Wondrous Love Is This

Anonymous

Southern Harmony, 1835
Wondrous Love

1. What won-drous love is this, oh, my soul, oh, my
2. When I was sink-ing down, sink-ing down, sink-ing
3. To God and to the Lamb, I will sing, I will
4. And when from death I'm free I'll sing on, I'll sing

soul, What won-drous love is this, oh, my soul; What
down, When I was sink-ing down, sink-ing down, When
sing, To God and to the Lamb, I will sing; To
on, And when from death I'm free I'll sing on, And

won-drous love is this That caused the Lord__ of
I was sink-ing down Be-neath God's right-eous
God and to the Lamb, Who is the great__ I
when from death I'm free I'll sing and joy-ful

bliss To bear the dread-ful curse for my soul, for my
frown Christ laid a-side His crown for my soul, for my
Am, While mil-lions join the theme, I will sing, I will
be, And thro' e-ter-ni-ty I'll sing on, I'll sing

soul, To bear the dread-ful curse for my soul.
soul, Christ laid a-side His crown for my soul.
sing, While mil-lions join the theme, I will sing.
on, And thro' e-ter-ni-ty I'll sing on.

God Is Love, by Him Upholden

J. S. B. Monsell

Peter Cutts
Wylde Green

1. God is love, by Him up-hold-en
Hang the glo-rious orbs of light, In their
lan-guage, glad and gold-en, Speak-ing
to us day and night Their great sto-ry,
God is love, and God is light.

2. Through that pre-cious love He sought us
Wan-dering from His ho-ly ways; With that
pre-cious life He bought us; Then let
all our fu-ture days Tell this sto-ry,
Love is life, our lives be praise.

3. Glad-some is the theme and glo-rious,
Praise to Christ our gra-cious Head; Christ, the
ris-en Christ, vic-tor-ious, Earth and
hell hath cap-tive led. Wel-come sto-ry!
Love lives on, and death is dead.

4. Up to Him let each af-fec-tion
Dai-ly rise and round Him move; Our whole
lives one res-ur-rec-tion To the
life of life a-bove; Their glad sto-ry,
God is life, and God is love.

48
Rejoice, Ye Pure in Heart

Edward H. Plumptre

Richard Dirksen
Vineyard Haven

1. Re - joice, ye pure in__ heart! Re - joice, give thanks,
2. With all the an - gel__ choirs, With__ all the saints
3. Your clear ho - san - nas__ raise, And__ al - le - lu -
4. Yes, on through life's long__ path, Still__ chant - ing as
5. Still lift your stan - dard__ high, Still__ march in firm
6. At last the march shall__ end; The__ wear - ied ones
7. Then on, ye pure in__ heart! Re - joice, give thanks,

1. and__ sing! Your__ glo - rious ban - ner wave__ on high,
2. of__ earth, Pour__ out the strains of joy__ and bliss,
3. ias__ loud; While__ ans - wer - ing ech - oes up - ward float,
4. ye__ go, From__ youth to age, by night__ and day,
5. ar - ray, As__ war - riors through the dark - ness toil,
6. shall rest; The__ pil - grims find their Fa - ther's house,
7. and__ sing! Your__ glo - rious ban - ner wave__ on high,

1. The__ cross of Christ, your__ King.
2. True rap - ture, no - blest__ mirth.
3. Like__ wreaths of in - cense__ cloud.
4. In__ glad - ness and in__ woe.
5. Till dawns the gold - en__ day.
6. Je - ru - sa - lem the__ blest.
7. The__ cross of Christ, your__ King.

Refrain

Ho - san - na, Ho - san - na, Re - joice,__ give__ thanks and sing.__

Cosmic Festival

49

Richard Felciano

A — Elizabeth Barrett Browning
Earth's crammed with heav-en and ev-'ry liv-ing thing a-fire with God.

B — Ralph Waldo Emerson
To the wise, life is a fes-ti-val.

C
Fes-ti-val, fes-ti-val, fes-ti-val, fes-ti-val.

D — Walt Whitman
Truth lies wait-ing in all things, un-fold-ing it-self from liv-ing buds. But it must be first in your-self. It shall come from your soul. It shall be love.

50 O God, Whose Will Is Life

Rolland W. Schloerb

Thomas Tallis

Third Mode Melody

1. O God, whose will is life and peace
   for all the sons of men, Let not our hu-
   man hates re - lease the sword's dread power a - gain.
   For - give our nar - row - ness of mind; des - troy
   false pride, we plead; De - li - ver us
   and all man - kind from sel - fish - ness and greed.

2. O God, whose ways shall lead to peace,
   en - light - en us, we pray; Dis - pel our dark -
   ness and in - crease the light a - long our way.
   Il - lu - mine those who lead the lands that they
   may make at length The laws of right
   to guide the hands that wield the na - tions' strength.

3. O God, who call - est us to peace,
   we join with ev - 'ry - one Who does his part
   that wars may cease and jus - tice may be done.
   En - a - ble us to take the way the Prince
   of Peace hath trod; Cre - ate the will
   to build each day the fa - mi - ly of God.

All My Hope on God
Is Founded

Robert Bridges
Based on the German of J. Neander

Herbert Howells
Michael

1. All my hope on God is found-ed; He doth still my
2. Pride of man and earth-ly glo-ry, Sword and crown be-
3. God's great good-ness aye en-dur-eth, Deep His wis-dom,
4. Dai-ly doth th'Al-might-y Gi-ver Boun-teous gifts on
5. Still from man to God e-ter-nal Sac-ri-fice of

1. trust re-new: Me through change and chance He
2. tray man's trust; What with care and toil he
3. pass-ing thought: Splen-dor, light and life at-
4. us be-stow; His de-sire our soul de-
5. praise be done, High a-bove all prais-es

1. guid-eth, On-ly good and on-ly true. God un-
2. build-eth, Tower and tem-ple, fall to dust. But God's
3. tend Him, Beau-ty spring-eth out of naught. Ev-er-
4. light-eth, Pleas-ure leads us where we go. Love doth
5. prais-ing, For the gift of Christ, His Son. Christ doth

1. known, He a-lone Calls my heart to be His own.
2. power, Hour by hour, Is my tem-ple and my tower.
3. more From His store New-born worlds rise and a-dore.
4. stand At His hand; Joy doth wait on His com-mand.
5. call One and all: Ye who fol-low shall not fall.

52 All Poor Men and Humble

Tr. from the Welsh by K. E. Roberts

M. Lee Suitor
Poverty

1. All poor men and hum-ble, All lame men who stum-ble, Come haste ye, nor feel ye a-fraid; For Je-sus our trea-sure, With love past all mea-sure, In low-ly poor man-ger was laid.

2. Though wise men who found Him Laid rich gifts a-round Him, Yet ox-en they gave Him their hay: And Je-sus in beau-ty ac-cept-ed their du-ty; Con-tent-ed in man-ger He lay.

3. Then haste we to show Him The prais-es we owe Him, Our ser-vice He ne'er can de-spise: Whose love is still a-ble to show us the sta-ble Where soft-ly in man-ger He lies.

As the Lyre

Narayan Vaman Tilak
Tr. by Nicol Macnicol

Chinese Melody
Adapt. by Austin C. Lovelace
China

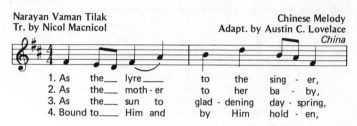

1. As the lyre to the sing - er,
2. As the moth - er to her ba - by,
3. As the sun to glad - dening day - spring,
4. Bound to Him and by Him hold - en,

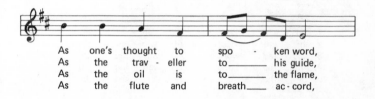

As one's thought to spo - ken word,
As the trav - eller to his guide,
As the oil is to the flame,
As the flute and breath ac - cord,

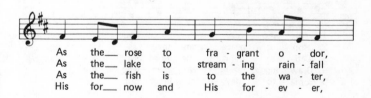

As the rose to fra - grant o - dor,
As the lake to stream - ing rain - fall
As the fish is to the wa - ter,
His for now and His for - ev - er,

So to me is Christ the Lord.
Stands the Sav - ior by my side.
So to me is His sweet name.
Is my soul to Christ the Lord.

54 All Who Love and Serve Your City

Erik Routley
Luke 19:41; Ezekiel 48:35

Peter Cutts
Birabus

1. All who love and serve your ci - ty,
2. In your day of loss and sor - row,
3. In your day of wealth and plen - ty,
4. For all days are days of judg - ment,
5. Ris - en Lord, shall yet the ci - ty,

1. All who bear its dai - ly stress,
2. In your day of help - less strife,
3. Was - ted work and was - ted play,
4. And the Lord is wait - ing still,
5. Be the ci - ty of des - pair?

1. All who cry for peace and jus - tice,
2. Hon - or, peace and love re - treat - ing,
3. Call to mind the word of Je - sus,
4. Draw - ing near to men who spurn him,
5. Come to - day, our Judge, our Glo - ry,

1. All who curse and all who bless.
2. Seek the Lord, who is your life.
3. 'Work ye yet while it is day.'
4. Off - ering peace from Cal - vary's hill.
5. Be its name, 'The Lord is there!'

All Who Love and Serve Your City

55

Erik Routley
Luke 19:41; Ezekiel 48:35

American Folk Tune
Charlestown

1. All who love and_ serve your ci - ty,
2. In your day of_ loss and sor - row,
3. In your day of_ wealth and plen - ty,
4. For all days are_ days of judg - ment,
5. Ris - en Lord, shall_ yet the ci - ty

1. All who_ bear its dai - ly stress,
2. In your_ day of help - less strife,
3. Was - ted_ work and was - ted play,
4. And the_ Lord is wait - ing still,
5. Be the_ ci - ty of des - pair?

1. All who_ cry for peace and jus - tice,
2. Hon - or,_ peace and love re - treat - ing,
3. Call to_ mind the word of Je - sus,
4. Draw - ing_ near to men who spurn him,
5. Come to - day, our Judge, our Glo - ry,

1. All who curse and all who bless.
2. Seek the Lord, who is your life.
3. 'Work ye yet while it is day.'
4. Off - ering peace from Cal - vary's hill.
5. Be its name, 'The Lord is there!'

56   An Alleluia Super-Round

William Albright

57

By Gracious Powers

Dietrich Bonhoeffer
Tr. by F. Pratt Green*

Joseph Gelineau

1. By gra - cious pow'rs so won - der - ful - ly shel - ter'd, and con - fi - dent - ly wait - ing come what may, We know that God is with us night and morn - ing and nev - er fails to greet us each new day.

2. Yet is this heart by its old foe tor - men - ted, still e - vil days bring bur - dens hard to bear; O give our fright - ened souls the sure sal - va - tion for which, O Lord, you taught us to pre - pare.

3. And when this cup you give is filled to brim - ming with bit - ter suf - fering, hard to un - der - stand, We take it thank - ful - ly and with - out trem - bling out of so good, and so be - loved a hand.

4. Yet when a - gain, in this same world you give us the joy we had, the bright - ness of your sun, We shall re - mem - ber all the days we lived through and our whole life shall then be yours a - lone.

*Verse 5 omitted.
Words used by permission of Oxford University Press.
Music used by permission of the Rev. Joseph Gelineau, Paris, France.

Christ the Worker

58

Tr. by Tom Colvin

Ghana Work Song

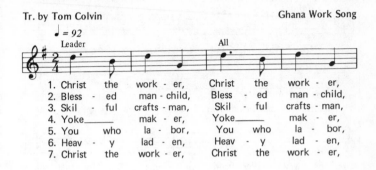

1. Christ the work - er, Christ the work - er,
2. Bless - ed man - child, Bless - ed man - child,
3. Skil - ful crafts - man, Skil - ful crafts - man,
4. Yoke___ mak - er, Yoke___ mak - er,
5. You who la - bor, You who la - bor,
6. Heav - y lad - en, Heav - y lad - en,
7. Christ the work - er, Christ the work - er,

1. born in Beth - le - hem, born to
2. boy of Naz - a - reth, grew in
3. bless - ed car - pen - ter, prais - ing
4. fash - ioned by His hands, eas - y
5. lis - ten to His call, He will
6. glad - ly come to Him, He will
7. God - in - Man,___ teach us

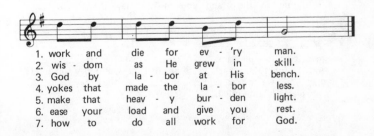

1. work and die for ev - 'ry man.
2. wis - dom as He grew in skill.
3. God by la - bor at His bench.
4. yokes that made the la - bor less.
5. make that heav - y bur - den light.
6. ease your load and give you rest.
7. how to do all work for God.

59 Divided Our Pathways

Christopher Coelho, O.F.M.   Christopher Coelho, O.F.M.

Refrain

Di - vid - ed our path - ways, and heav - y our guilt; bur - den'd, un - see - ing, we grope for the one way. Far from our home, O Fa - ther, we call out 'Heal us, for - give us: bring us to - geth - er in Je - sus your Son!'

Fine

Cantor

1. Holy Father, keep those you have giv - en me true to your Name, so___ that they may_____
2. Father, may they be one in us as you are in me and I am in you, so that the world may come to be-
3. I have given them the glo - ry that you gave to me, that___ they may_____
4. With me in them and you in me may they be so com - plete - ly u - nited, *(to 4.)*

lieve	all	be	one	as	we	are	one.
	it	was	you	who	sent	me.
	all	be	one	as	we	are	one.

(4.) that the world may know that it was you who sent me,

and that you love them as much as you love me.

60
As We Break the Bread

Fred Kaan

Stanley L. Osborne
Masson

1. As we break the bread and taste the life of wine,
2. Grain is sown to die; it ri - ses from the dead,
3. Pass from hand to hand the liv - ing love of Christ!
4. Je - sus binds in one our dai - ly life and work;
5. Hav - ing shared the bread that died to rise a - gain,

1. We bring to mind our Lord, man of all time.
2. Be - comes through hu - man toil our com-mon bread.
3. Ma - chine and man pro - vide bread for this feast.
4. He is of all man - kind sym - bol and mark.
5. We rise to serve the world, scat-tered as grain.

61

Sing of Mary

Anonymous c. 1914

American Folk Tune
Pleading Savior

1. Sing of Mary, pure and lowly, Virgin mother undefiled. Sing of God's own Son most holy, Who became her little child. Fairest child of fairest mother, God the Lord who

2. Sing of Jesus, Son of Mary, In the home at Nazareth. Toil and labor cannot weary Love enduring unto death. Constant was the love He gave her, Though He went forth

3. Glory be to God the Father; Glory be to God the Son; Glory be to God the Spirit; Glory to the Three in One From the heart of blessed Mary, From all saints the

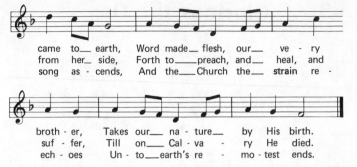

came to__ earth, Word made__ flesh, our__ ve-ry
from her__ side, Forth to__ preach, and__ heal, and
song as-cends, And the__ Church the__ strain re-

broth-er, Takes our__ na-ture__ by His birth.
suf-fer, Till on__ Cal-va-ry He died.
ech-oes Un-to__ earth's re-mo-test ends.

Beneath the Forms of Outward Rite

62

James A. Blaisdell

Leo Sowerby
Perry

1. Be - neath the forms of out-ward rite Thy
2. The bread is al - ways con-se-crate Which
3. The bless-ed cup is on - ly passed True
4. O Mas - ter, through these sym-bols shared, Thine

sup-per, Lord, is spread In ev-ery qui-et
men di-vide with men; And ev-ery act of
mem-o-ry of thee, When life a-new pours
own dear self im-part, That in our dai-ly

up-per room Where faint-ing souls are fed.
broth-er-hood Re-peats thy feast a - gain.
out its wine With rich suf-fi-cien-cy.
life may flame The pas-sion of thy heart.

63   Glorious the Day

F. Pratt Green

John Gardner
Ilfracombe

1. Glor-ious the day when Christ was born____
2. Glor-ious the day when Christ a - rose,____
3. Glor-ious the days of gos-pel grace____
4. Glor-ious the day when Christ ful-fils____

Al-le-lu-ia, Al-le-lu-ia, Al-le-lu - ia!

To wear the crown that Cae - sars scorn,____
The sur - est Friend of all His foes;____
When Christ re - stores the fall - en race;____
What man re - jects yet fee - bly wills;____

Al-le-lu-ia, Al-le-lu-ia, Al-le-lu - ia!

Whose life and death that love re - veal,____
Who for the sake of those He grieves____
When doubt - ers kneel and wa - verers stand,____
When that strong Light puts out the sun____

Al-le-lu-ia, Al-le-lu-ia, Al-le-lu - ia!

Which all men need and need to feel.
Tran-scends the world He nev-er leaves.
And faith a-chieves what rea-son planned.
And all is end-ed, all be-gun.

Al-le-lu-ià, Al-le-lu-ia, Al-le-lu-ia!

64

Beyond the Mist and Doubt

Donald Hughes

Erik Routley
Maiden Way

1. Be-yond the mist and doubt Of this un-cer-tain
(2.) rest-less in-tel-lect Has all things in its
(3.) in hu-mil-i-ty We know Thee by Thy

day, I trust in Thine e-ter-nal name, Be-
shade, But still to Thee my spir-it clings, Se-
grace, For sci-ence's re-mot-est probe Feels

1,2.

yond all chan-ges still the same, And in that
rene be-yond all shak-en things, And I am
but the frin-ges of Thy robe:

3.

name I pray.   2. Our
not a-fraid.   3. Still

Love looks up-on Thy face.

65 Jesus, We Want to Meet

A. T. Olajide Olude
Tr. by Biodun Adebesin
Versed by Austin C. Lovelace

A. T. Olajide Olude
Nigeria

1. Je - sus, we want to meet On this thy
2. We kneel in awe and fear On this thy
3. Thy bless - ing, Lord, we seek On this thy
4. Our minds we ded - i - cate On this thy

ho - ly day; We gath - er round thy throne
ho - ly day; Pray God to teach us here
ho - ly day; Give joy of thy vic - to - ry
ho - ly day; Heart and soul con - se - crate

On this thy ho - ly day. Thou art our
On this thy ho - ly day; Save us and
On this thy ho - ly day. Through grace a - lone
On this thy ho - ly day. Ho - ly Spir - it,

heaven - ly Friend, Hear our prayers as they as - cend;
cleanse our hearts, Lead and guide our acts of praise,
are we saved; In thy flock may we be found;
make us whole; Bless the ser - mon in this place;

Look in - to our hearts and minds to - day,
And our faith from seed to flow - er raise,
Let the mind of Christ a - bide in us
And as we go, lead us Lord;

Optional drumbeat patterns:

On   this___   thy   ho - ly   day.
On   this___   thy   ho - ly   day.
On   this___   thy   ho - ly   day.
We   shall be thine   ev - er - more.

66

Christ Is the World's Light

F. Pratt Green

Hungarian Carol
Christus Urunknak

1. Christ is   the world's light,   He   and none oth - er;
2. Christ is   the world's peace,   He   and none oth - er;
3. Christ is   the world's life,   He   and none oth - er;
4. Give   God the glo - ry,   God   and none oth - er!

Born   in our dark - ness,   He be - came our broth - er;
No   man can serve Him   and de - spise his broth - er;
Sold   once for sil - ver,   mur - dered here, our broth - er —
Give   God the glo - ry,   Spi - rit, Son, and Fa - ther!

If   we have seen Him,   we have seen the
Who   else u - nites us,   one in God   the
He,   who re - deems us,   reigns with God the
Give   God the glo - ry,   God in man my

Fa - ther;   Glo - ry to God on high.
Fa - ther?   Glo - ry to God on high.
Fa - ther: Glo - ry to God on high.
broth - er!   Glo - ry to God on high.

67

Christ, upon the Mountain Peak

Brian Wren

Peter Cutts
Shillingford

1. Christ, up-on the moun-tain peak
2. Trem-bling at His feet we saw
3. Swift the cloud of glo-ry came,
4. This is God's be-lov-ed Son!

stands a-lone in glo-ry blaz-ing;
Mo-ses and E-li-jah speak-ing.
God pro-claim-ing in its thun-der
Law and pro-phets fade be-fore Him;

Let us, if we dare to speak,
All the pro-phets and the law
Je-sus as His Son by name!
First and last and on-ly one,

with the saints and an-gels
shout through them their joy-ful
Na-tions, cry a-loud in
let cre-a-tion now a-

praise Him.
greet-ing.
won-der — Al-le-lu-ia!
dore Him.

Christ Is Alive

68

Brian A. Wren

Psalmodia Evangelica
Truro
Descant by Alastair Cassels-Brown

Descant: Al - le - lu - ia, Al - le - lu - ia, Al - le - lu - ia, Al - le - lu - ia, Al - le - lu - ia, Al - le - lu - ia, Al - le - lu - ia, Al - le - lu - ia.

1. Christ is a - live! Let Chris - tians sing. His cross stands emp - ty to the sky. Let streets and homes with prais - es ring. His love in death shall nev - er die.

2. Christ is a - live! No long - er bound To dis - tant years in Pal - es - tine, He comes to claim the here and now. And con - quer ev - ery place and time.

3. Not throned a - bove, re - mote - ly high, Un - touched, un - moved by hu - man pains, But dai - ly, in the midst of life, Our Sa - vior with the Fa - ther reigns.

4. Christ is a - live! As - cend - ant Lord, He rules the world His Fa - ther made, Till in the end His love a - dored, Shall be to ev - ery man dis - played.

69

Come, Risen Lord

G.W. Briggs

Alfred M. Smith
Sursum Corda

1. Come, ris - en Lord, and deign to be our guest; Nay,
2. We meet, as in that up - per room they met, Thou
3. One bod - y we, one bod - y who par - take, One
4. One with each oth - er, Lord, for one in Thee, Who

let us be Thy guests; the feast is Thine; Thy -
at the ta - ble, bless - ing, yet dost stand; "This
church u - nit - ed in com - mu - nion blest; One
art one Sav - ior and one liv - ing Head; Then

self at Thine own board make man - i - fest In
is my bod - y;" so Thou giv - est yet: Faith
name we bear, one bread of life we break, With
o - pen Thou our eyes, that we may see; Be

this our Sac - ra - ment of bread and wine.
still re - ceives the cup as from Thy hand.
all Thy saints on earth and saints at rest.
known to us in break - ing of the bread.

Words from ENLARGED SONGS OF PRAISE by permission of Oxford University Press.
Music Copyright by Alfred M. Smith. Used by permission of Mrs. Alfred M. Smith.

Down to Earth 70

Fred Kaan

Austin C. Lovelace
Inwood

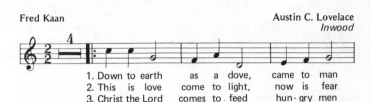

1. Down to earth as a dove, came to man
2. This is love come to light, now is fear
3. Christ the Lord comes to feed hun-gry men

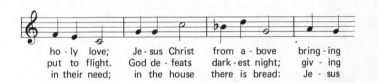

ho - ly love; Je - sus Christ from a - bove bring-ing
put to flight. God de-feats dark-est night; giv-ing
in their need; in the house there is bread: Je - sus

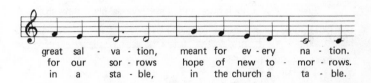

great sal - va - tion, meant for ev-ery na - tion.
for our sor - rows hope of new to - mor - rows.
in a sta - ble, in the church a ta - ble.

Let us sing, sing, sing, Dance and spring, spring, spring.

St. 3 small notes

Christ is here, ev - er near! Glo - ria in ex - cel - sis.

71 Come Sunday

Duke Ellington   Duke Ellington

(Chorus) Oo_____ Oo_____ Come

Sun-day, oh come Sun-day, That's the day._____

(Solo) Lord, Dear Lord a - bove: God Al - might - y; God of

love, Please look down and see my peo - ple through.__

(Chorus) 1. I be - lieve that God put sun and
2. Heav - en is a good - ness time. A
3. I be - lieve God is now, was then

moon up in the sky. I don't mind the
bright - er light on high. *(Spoken)* Do unto others as you would
and al - ways will be. With God's bless - ing

gray skies, 'cause they're just clouds pass - ing
have them do to you, *(Sung)* and have a bright - er
we can make it through e - ter - ni-

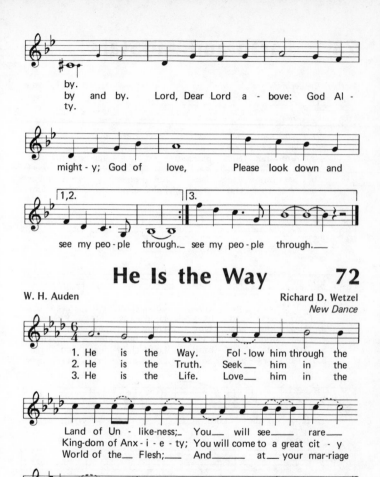

by.
by. and by. Lord, Dear Lord a - bove: God Al -
ty.

might - y; God of love, Please look down and

1,2.
see my peo - ple through. 3. see my peo - ple through.

He Is the Way 72

W. H. Auden

Richard D. Wetzel
New Dance

1. He is the Way. Fol - low him through the
2. He is the Truth. Seek him in the
3. He is the Life. Love him in the

Land of Un - like-ness; You will see rare
King-dom of Anx - i - e - ty; You will come to a great cit - y
World of the Flesh; And at your mar-riage

beasts, and have u - nique ad - ven - tures.
that has ex - pect - ed your re-turn for years.
all its oc - ca - sions shall dance for joy.

73   Earth and All Stars

Herbert Brokering

David N. Johnson
Dexter

1. Earth and all stars, Loud rush-ing plan-ets
2. Hail, wind and rain, Loud blow-ing snow-storm
3. Trum-pet and pipes, Loud clash-ing cym-bals
4. Ma-chines and steel, Loud pound-ing ham-mers
5. Class-rooms and labs, Loud boil-ing test-tubes
6. Knowl-edge and truth, Loud sound-ing wis-dom

Sing to the Lord_____ a new song!

1. O vic-to-ry, Loud shout-ing ar-my
2. Flow-ers and trees, Loud rus-tling dry leaves
3. Harp, lute and lyre, Loud hum-ming cel-los
4. Lime-stone and beams, Loud build-ing work-men
5. Ath-lete and band, Loud cheer-ing peo-ple
6. Daugh-ter and son, Loud pray-ing mem-bers

Sing to the Lord_____ a new song!

Refrain

He hath done mar - vel-ous things.

I, too, will praise Him with a new song!

From TWELVE FOLKSONGS AND SPIRITUALS © 1968, Augsburg Publishing House, Minneapolis, Minnesota. Used by permission.

Faith While Trees Are Still in Blossom

Anders Frostenson
Tr. by Fred Kaan

Alec Wyton
Faith

1. Faith, while trees are still in blos - som, plans the pick - ing of the fruit; faith can feel the thrill of har - vest when the buds be - gin to sprout.
2. Long be - fore the dawn is break - ing, faith an - ti - ci - pates the sun. Faith is ea - ger for the day - light, for the work that must be done.
3. Long be - fore the rains were com - ing Noah went and built an ark. A - bra - ham, the lone - ly mi - grant, saw the Light be - yond the dark.
4. Faith, up - lift - ed, tamed the wa - ter of the un - di - vid - ed sea, and the peo - ple of the He - brews found the path that made them free.
5. Faith be - lieves that God is faith - ful, He will be that He will be! Faith ac - cepts His call, re - spond - ing: 'I am will - ing, Lord, send me.'

75 God in His Love

F. Pratt Green

Austin C. Lovelace
Ecology

1. God in His love for us___ lent us this
2. Thanks be to God___ for its bount - y and
3. Long have the wars of man___ ruined his___
4. Cas - ual de - spoil - ers, or high - priests of
5. Earth is the Lord's:___ it is ours to en -

1. plan - et, Gave it a pur - pose in
2. beau - ty, Life that sus - tains___ us in
3. har - vest; Long has Earth bowed___ to the
4. Mam - mon Sell - ing the fu - ture for
5. joy___ it, Ours, as His stew - ards, to

1. time___ and in space; Small as a spark___
2. bod - y and mind: Plen - ty for all,___
3. ter - ror of force. Now we pol - lute___
4. pre - sent re - wards, Care - less of life___
5. farm___ and de - fend. Now from pol - lu -

1. from the fire of cre - a - tion, Cra - dle of
2. if we learn how to share___ it, Rich - es un -
3. it, in cyn - i - cal si - lence: Poi - son the
4. and con - temp - tuous of beau - ty: Bid us re -
5. tion, dis - ease, and dam - na - tion, Good Lord, de -

1. life___ and the   home___ of   our   race.
2. dreamed of   to   fath - om and   find.
3. foun - tain of   life___ at   its   source.
4. mem - ber: the   Earth___ is   the   Lord's!
5. liv - er us,___   world___ with - out end!

Christian People, 76
Raise Your Song

Colin Thompson

Leisentritt's Gesangbuch, 1584
Ave Virgo Virginum

1. Chris - tian peo - ple,   raise your song,   Chase a - way all
   Sing your joy and   be made strong   Our Lord's life re -
2. Come to wel - come Christ to - day,   God's great re - ve -
   He has pi - o - neered the way   Of the new cre -

griev - ing.
ceiv - ing.   1. Na - ture's gifts of   wheat and vine
la - tion.   2. Greet Him, Christ our   ris - en King
a - tion.

Now are set be - fore us: As we of - fer
Glad - ly rec - og - niz - ing,   As with joy men

bread and wine   Christ comes to re - store us.
greet the spring   Out of win - ter ris - ing.

77 Fill Us with Your Love

Tr. by Tom Colvin

Ghana Folk Song

Chorus

Je - su,_____ Je - su,_____ Fill
us with Your love, show us how to serve the
neigh - bors we have from You._____

Verse

1. Kneels at the feet of His friends,
2. Neigh - bors are rich men and poor,
3. These are the ones we should serve,
4. Lov - ing puts us on our knees,

1. Si - lent - ly wash - es their feet, Mas - ter who
2. Neigh - bors are black men and white, Neigh - bors are
3. These are the ones we should love. All men are
4. Serv - ing as though we are slaves, This is the

1. acts as a slave_____ to them.
2. near - by and far_____ a - way.
3. neigh - bors to us_____ and You.
4. way we should live_____ with You.

Thank You, Lord, for Water, Soil and Air

78

Brian Wren

Erik Routley
Althorp

1. Thank you, Lord, for wa - ter, soil and air —
2. Thank you, Lord, for mi - ne - rals and ores-
3. Thank you, Lord, for price - less e - ner - gy
4. Thank you, Lord, for weav - ing na - ture's life
5. Thank you, Lord, for mak - ing pla - net earth

1. large gifts sup - port - ing ev' - ry - thing___ that
2. the ba - sis of all build - ing, wealth___ and
3. stored in each a - tom, ga - thered from___ the
4. in - to a seam - less robe,___ a fra - gile
5. a home for us and a - ges yet___ un -

1. lives.___ For - give___ our spoil - ing and a - buse of them.___
2. speed.___ For - give___ our reck - less plun - der - ing and waste.___
3. sun.___ For - give___ our greed and care - less - ness of power.___
4. whole.___ For - give___ our haste that tam - pers un - a - wares.___
5. born.___ — Help us to share, con - si - der, save and store.___

1,2,3,4 | 5.

1. Help us re - new___ the face of the earth.
2. Help us re - new___ the face of the earth.
3. Help us re - new___ the face of the earth.
4. Help us re - new___ the face of the earth.
5. Come and re - new___ the face of the earth.___

79 God of Love

Timothy Rees

Herbert Murrill
Carolyn

1. God of love and truth and beau-ty, hal-lowed be Thy name; Fóunt of or-der, law, and du-ty, hal-lowed be Thy name. As in heaven Thy hosts a-dore Thee, And their fa-ces veil be-fore Thee, So on earth, Lord, we im-plore Thee, hal-lowed be Thy name.

2. Lord, re-move our guil-ty blind-ness, hal-lowed be Thy name; Show Thy heart of lov-ing kind-ness, hal-lowed be Thy name. By our heart's deep-felt con-tri-tion, By our mind's en-light-ened vi-sion, By our will's com-plete sub-mis-sion, hal-lowed be Thy name.

3. In our wor-ship, Lord most ho-ly, hal-lowed be Thy name; In our work, how-ev-er low-ly, hal-lowed be Thy name. In each heart's im-ag-i-na-tion, In the Chur-ch's a-do-ra-tion, In the con-science of the na-tion, hal-lowed be Thy name

God, Who Spoke
in the Beginning

Fred Kaan

Erik Routley
Corbridge

1. God who spoke in the be-gin-ning,
2. God who spoke through men and na-tions,
3. God whose speech be-comes in-car-nate,

form - ing rock and shap - ing spar, set all
through e - vents long past and gone; show - ing
Christ is ser - vant, Christ is Lord! calls us

life and growth in mo - tion, earth - ly world and
still to - day His pur - pose, speaks su - preme - ly
to a life of ser - vice, heart and will to

dis - tant star; He who calls the earth to or - der
through His Son; He who calls the earth to or - der
ac - tion stirred; He who us - es man's o - be-dience

is the ground of what_____ we are.
gives His word and it_____ is done.
has the first and fi_____ nal word.

81 God Who Stretched the Spangled Heavens

Catherine Cameron

American Folk Tune
Holy Manna

1. God, who stretched the span - gled hea - vens,
2. Proud - ly rise our mod - ern cit - ies,
3. We have con - quered worlds un-dreamed of
4. As Thy new hor - i - zons beck - on,

In - fi - nite in time and place,
State - ly build - ings, row on row;
Since the child - hood of our race;
Fa - ther, give us strength to be

Flung the suns in burn - ing ra - diance
Yet their win - dows, blank, un - feel - ing,
Known the ec - sta - sy of wing - ing
Chil - dren of cre - a - tive pur - pose,

Through the si - lent fields of space.
Stare on can - yoned streets be - low,
Known un - char - ted realms of space,
Think - ing Thy thoughts af - ter Thee,

We Thy child - ren, in Thy_ like - ness,
Where the lone - ly drift un - no - ticed
Probed the se - crets of the_ a - tom,
Till our dreams are rich with_ mean - ing,

Share in - ven - tive powers with_ Thee:
In the cit - y's ebb and_ flow,
Yield - ing un - im - a - gined_ power,
Each en - deav - or, Thy de - sign:

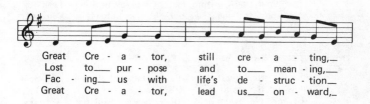

Great Cre - a - tor, still cre - a - ting,_
Lost to_ pur - pose and to_ mean - ing,_
Fac - ing_ us with life's de - struc - tion_
Great Cre - a - tor, lead us_ on - ward,_

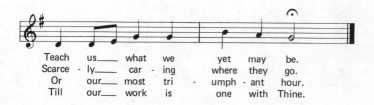

Teach us_ what we yet may be.
Scarce - ly_ car - ing where they go.
Or our_ most tri - umph - ant hour.
Till our_ work is one with Thine.

82   Good Spirit of God

Didier Rimaud
Tr. by Erik Routley

Jean van de Cauter
Good Spirit

1. Good Spirit of God, guide of your chil-dren,
2. Pure Spirit of God, fresh wind of bless-ing,
3. Great Spirit of God, source of all jus-tice,

Keep them all for the glo-ry of the Fa-ther;
Let your fire in its en-er-gy in-flame us;
In your war a-gainst ha-tred keep us faith-ful;

Keep them all in the love of one an-oth-er; Lead them
Let your heal-ing from mis-er-y re-claim us; Lead us
In pro-tect-ing the poor keep us watch-ful; In our

all in the quest for the hon-or of the king-dom.
all where the faith-ful Christ's grace are con-fess-ing.
search for the house-hold of peace still pro-tect us.

Be our guide through this pil-grim-age of liv-ing,

Turn us each to his broth-er in self-giv-ing.

If You Have Ears 83

Fred Kaan

Alec Wyton
Listen

1. If you have ears, then lis-ten to what the
3. If you have buds for tast-ing the ap-ple
5. If you can smell the per-fume of life, the

1. Spir-it says and give an o-pen hear-ing to
3. of God's eye, then go, en-joy cre-a-tion and
5. feast of earth, then sow the seeds of laugh-ter and

1. won-der and sur-prise. 2. If you have eyes for
3. peo-ple on the way. 4. If you have hands for
5. tend the shoots of mirth. 6. Come, peo-ple, to your

2. hear-ing the word in hu-man form, then
4. car-ing, then pray that you may know the
6. sen-ses and cel-e-brate the day! For

2. let your love be tell-ing and
4. ten-der art of lov-ing our
6. God gives wine for wa-ter, the

verse 2, 4 | last verse

2. your com-pass-ion warm.
4. world of touch and go.
6. gift of light for grey.

84 I Come with Joy

Brian Wren

American Folk Tune
Dove of Peace
Arr. Austin C. Lovelace

1. I come with joy to meet my Lord, For-
2. I come with Christ - ians far and near To
3. As Christ breaks bread for men to share Each
4. And thus with joy we meet our Lord. His
5. To - geth - er met, to - geth - er bound, We'll

1. giv - en, loved and free,___ In awe and won - der
2. find, as we are fed,___ Man's true com - mun - i -
3. proud di - vi - sion ends.___ The love that made__ us,
4. pres - ence, al - ways near,___ Is in such friend- ship
5. go our dif - f'rent ways,___ And as His peo - ple

1. to re - call His life laid down___ for
2. ty of love In Christ's com - mun - ion
3. makes us one, And stran - gers now___ are
4. bet - ter known; We see and praise___ Him
5. in the world, We'll live and speak___ His

1. me,___ His life laid down__ for me.___
2. bread,___ In Christ's com - mun - ion bread.___
3. friends,___ And stran - gers now___ are friends.___
4. here;___ We see and praise__ Him here.___
5. praise,___ We'll live and speak__ His praise.___

Now Let Us
from This Table Rise

Fred Kaan

Grenoble Antiphoner, 1753
Deus Tuorum Militum

1. Now let us from this ta - ble rise re -
2. With minds a - lert, up - held by grace, to
3. To fill each hu - man house with love, it
4. Then grant us cou - rage, Fa - ther God, to

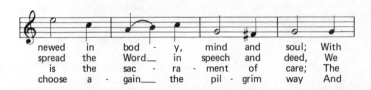

newed in bod - y, mind and soul; With
spread the Word in speech and deed, We
is the sac - ra - ment of care; The
choose a - gain the pil - grim way And

Christ we die and live a - gain, His
fol - low in the steps of Christ, at
work that Christ be - gan to do we
help us to ac - cept with joy the

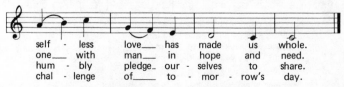

self - less love has made us whole.
one with man in hope and need.
hum - bly pledge our - selves to share.
chal - lenge of to - mor - row's day.

86 In Christ There Is No East or West

John Oxenham

Ned Rorem
No East or West

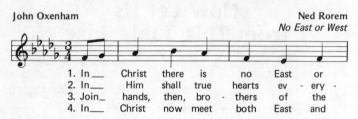

1. In__ Christ there is no East or
2. In__ Him shall true hearts ev - ery -
3. Join__ hands, then, bro - thers of the
4. In__ Christ now meet both East and

West, In__ Him no South__ or
where Their__ high__ com - mun - ion
faith, What - e'er__ your race__ may
West, In__ him__ meet South__ and

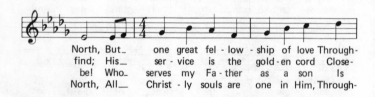

North, But__ one great fel - low - ship of love Through-
find; His__ ser - vice is the gold - en cord Close-
be! Who__ serves my Fa - ther as a son Is
North, All__ Christ - ly souls are one in Him, Through-

out the whole wide earth.
bind - ing all man - kind.
sure - ly kin to me.
out the whole wide earth. A - men.

Lord, As We Rise   87

Fred Kaan

Erik Routley
Wansbeck

1. Lord, as we rise to leave this shell of worship, Call'd to the risk of unprotected living, Willing to be at one with all your people, We ask for courage.

2. For all the strain with living interwoven, For the demands each day will make upon us, And for the love we owe the modern city, Lord, make us cheerful.

3. Give us an eye for openings to serve you; Make us alert when calm is interrupted, Ready and wise to use the unexpected; Sharpen our insight.

4. Lift from our life the blanket of convention: Give us the nerve to lose our life to others. Be with your church in death and resurrection: Lord of all ages.

88 Lord Christ When First Thou Cam'st to Men

Walter Russell Bowie

Ludwig M. Lindeman
Kirken den er et gammelt hus

1. Lord Christ when first Thou cam'st to men
Up - on a cross_ they bound Thee,
And mock'd Thy sav - ing king - ship then
By thorns with which_ they crowned Thee:
And still our wrongs may weave Thee now

2. O awe - ful love which found no room
In life where sin_ de - nied Thee,
And, doom'd to death, must bring to doom
The power which cru - ci - fied Thee,
Till not a stone was left on stone,

3. New ad - vent of the love of Christ,
Shall we a - gain_ re - fuse Thee,
Till in the night of hate and war
We per - ish as_ we lose Thee?
From old un - faith our souls re - lease

4. O wound - ed hands of Je - sus, build
In us Thy new_ cre - a - tion;
Our pride is dust, our vaunt is stilled,
We wait thy rev - e - la - tion;
O love that tri - umphs o - ver loss,

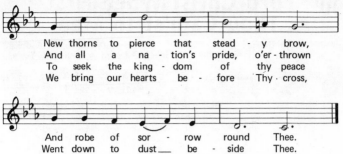

New thorns to pierce that stead - y brow,
And all a na - tion's pride, o'er - thrown
To seek the king - dom of thy peace
We bring our hearts be - fore Thy cross,

And robe of sor - row round Thee.
Went down to dust___ be - side Thee.
By which a - lone___ we choose Thee.
To fin - ish Thy___ sal - va - tion.

Strengthen for Service 89

Syriac, Liturgy of Malabar
Tr. by C. W. Humphreys
Alt. by Percy Dearmer

David McK. Williams
Malabar

1. Strength-en for serv - ice, Lord, the hands That ho - ly
2. Lord, may the tongues which "Ho- ly" sang, Keep free from
3. The feet that tread Thy hal-lowed courts From light do

things have tak - en; Let ears that now have heard Thy
all de - ceiv - ing; The eyes which saw Thy love be
Thou not ban - ish; The bod - ies by Thy bod - y

songs To clam - or nev - er wak - en.
bright, Thy bless - ed hope per - ceiv - ing.
fed With Thy new life re - plen - ish.

Alt. by Percy Dearmer from SONGS OF PRAISE by permission of Oxford University Press.
Music used by permission of the Church Pension Fund.

90 Men Go to God

Dietrich Bonhoeffer
Tr. by Geoffrey Winthrop Young

Melchior Vulpius
Hinunter ist der Sonne
Melody Adapted by Carlton R. Young

1. Men go to__ God when they are sore be-stead,
   Pray to Him for suc-cour,__ for His peace, for
   bread, For mer-cy for__ them, the__
   sick,__ sin-ning, or dead; All men do so,
   Christ-ian and un-be-liev-ing.

2. Men go to__ God when He is sore be-stead,
   Find Him poor and scorned with-out shel-ter__ or
   bread, — Whelmed__ un-der__ weight of the
   wick-ed, the weak, the__ dead; Christ-ians stand by
   God__ in His hour of griev-ing.

3. God go-eth to ev-ery man when sore be-stead,
   Feed-eth bo-dy and__ the__ spir-it with His
   bread. For Christ-ians, pa-gans a-like He__
   hang-eth__ dead, And__ both a-
   like__ for-giv-ing.__

Now the Silence

91

Jaroslav J. Vajda

Carl Schalk
Now

Now the si - lence Now the peace Now the emp- ty

hands___ up - lift - ed Now the kneel - ing Now the plea

Now the Fa - ther's arms___ in wel-come Now the hear-ing Now

the power Now the ves - sel brimmed___ for pour - ing

Now the bod - y Now the blood Now the joy - ful

cel - e - bra - tion Now the wed-ding Now the songs

Now the heart for - giv - en leap - ing Now the

Spir - it's vis - i - ta - tion Now the Son's e -

piph - a - ny Now the Fa - ther's bless - ing Now

92 Now Join We to Praise the Creator*

Fred Kaan

Austin C. Lovelace
Sharing

1. Now join we to praise the Cre - a - tor, Our voic - es in wor-ship and song;_____ We stand to re-call with thanks-giv - ing That to Him all sea - sons be - long._____ We thank you, O God, for your good - ness, For the joy and a - bun-dance of crops,_____ For

2. But al - so of need and star - va - tion We sing with con-cern and de - spair,_____ Of skills that are used for de - struc - tion, Of land that is burnt and laid bare._____ We cry for the plight of the hun - gry, While__ har - vests are left in the field,_____ For

3. The song grows in depth and in wide - ness; The earth and the peo - ple are one._____ There can be no thanks with - out giv - ing, No words with - out deeds that are done._____ Then teach us, O Lord of the har - vest, To be hum - ble in all that we claim,_____ To

food that is stored in the cup - boards, For
or - chards neg - lect - ed and wast - ing, For
share what we have with the na - tions, To

all we can buy in the shops.____
pro - duce from mar - kets with - held.____
care for the world in your name.____

93

We Thank You, God

Frances Hill West

Gerald Wheeler
Emery

1. We thank you, God, for soft green grass and
2. We thank you, God, for o - cean tides, and
3. We thank you, God, for qui - et nights, and
4. We thank you, God, for thoughts of men, and

bud - ding leaves, for sim - ple mu - sic
clear, salt air, for ships that sail a -
stars that shine, for or - der in this
deeds of worth, for those whose lives and

of the wind through sway - ing trees.
cross the waves with car - goes rare.
un - i - verse of your de - sign.
love re - veal your will on earth.

94

O Jesus Christ,
to You May Hymns

Bradford Webster

Daniel Moe
City of God

1. O Je - sus Christ, to you may hymns be
2. Show us your Spir - it, brood - ing o'er each
3. Grant us new cou - rage, sac - ri - fi - cial,

ris - ing, In ev - ery cit - y for your
cit - y, As you once wept a - bove Je -
hum - ble, Strong in your strength to ven - ture

love and care; In - spire our wor - ship,
ru - sa - lem, Seek - ing to gath - er
and to dare; To lift the fall - en,

grant the glad sur - pris - ing That your blest
all in love and pit - y, And heal - ing
guide the feet that stum - ble, Seek out the

Spir - it brings men ev - ery - where.
those who touch your gar - ment's hem.
lone - ly and God's mer - cy share.

Our Father, Whose Creative Will

95

W. H. Auden

Alec Wyton
Auden

1. Our Fa - ther, whose cre - a - tive will Asked
(2.) writ - ten by Thy chil - dren with A
(3.) flict Thy prom - is - es with each Oc -

be - ing for us all,___ Con - firm it that Thy
smudged and crook - ed line,___ The word is ev - er
ca - sion of dis - tress,___ That from our in - co -

pri - mal love May weave in us the
leg - i - ble, Thy mean - ing un - e -
her - ence we May learn to put our

free - dom of The ac - tual - ly de -
quiv - o - cal, And for Thy good - ness
trust in Thee, And brut - al fact per -

fi - cient on The just - ly ac - tu -
e - ven sin Is val - id as a
suade us to Ad - ven - ture, art and

1,2.

3.

al. 2. Though
sign. 3. In -

peace. A men.

96 Sing God a Simple Song

Stephen Schwartz and Leonard Bernstein

Leonard Bernstein
From: "MASS"

Sing God a sim- ple song: Lau - da, Lau -
dē Make it up___ as you go a - long:
Lau - da, Lau - dē Sing like you like to sing.
God loves all sim - ple things, For God is the
sim - plest of all, For God is the
sim - plest of all._____
I will sing the Lord a
new___ song___ To praise Him, to bless Him, to

Our Jesus Is Savior   97

Traditional Cameroun Melody
Easter Song

Abel Nkuinji
Tr. by Erik Routley

Arranged by A. J. Tetouom

1. Our Je-sus is Sav-ior,___ Lord and friend;
2. The cit-y re-joic-es, the chil-dren sing:
3. The Ta-ble is set in an up-per room:
4. In form of a ser-vant He wash-es their feet,
5. They all go with Him to Geth-se-ma-ne,
6. 'Not guil-ty,' says Pi-late, and wash-es his hands.
7. Be-fore eve-ning falls, it___ all___ is done;
8. Where are the dis-ci-ples? where now are His friends?
9. Two nights and a day, and the news is a-broad:
10. So praise we God's love for what Je-sus has done.

1. He searched all our life from___ end to end. *(Refrain A)*
2. 'A day___ of joy: be-hold our King!' *(Refrain B)*
3. the bread and the wine fore-tell his doom. *(Refrain A)*
4. and says___ 'Thus hum-bly each oth-er greet.' *(Refrain A)*
5. but in Pi-late's courts there is none but He. *(Refrain A)*
6. 'A-way with Him now!' the___ crowd de-mands. *(Refrain A)*
7. the tomb___ re-ceives our___ ho-ly One. *(Refrain B)*
8. The Lord___ is dead: and here all hope ends. *(No Refrain)*
9. Not end but be-gin-ning! A-live is the Lord! *(Refrain B 2x)*
10. Now death is de-feat-ed, and vic-to-ry won. *(Refrain B)*

Refrain

(A) And he came down to earth___ to shed his blood on
(B) Sing___ al-le-lu-ia,___ for Christ the Lord is

Cal-va-ry, all to give life___ to men.
ri-sen, all to give life___ to men.

98 Praise to God

Traditional Russian
Tr. by Percy Dearmer

Yakushkin (1815)
Rasumovsky
Arr. by Ronald Arnatt

1. Praise to God in the high-est! Bless us, O Fa-ther! Praise to Thee.
2. Guide and pros-per the na-tions, ru-lers and peo-ple: Praise to Thee.
7. Peace on earth, and good-will, be ev-er a-mong us: Praise to Thee.

3. May the truth in its beau-ty flour-ish tri-um-phant: Praise to Thee.

S.A.T.B. Melody in the Bass

4. May the mills___ bring us bread, ___ for

food and for giv - ing: Praise___ to ___ Thee.

A.T.B.

5. May the good___ be o - beyed, ___ and

ev - il be___ con - quered: Praise___ to Thee.

S.A.T.B. Melody in the Alto

6. Give us laugh - ter, and set___ us

D.C. for Verse 7

gai - ly re - joic - ing: Praise___ to___ Thee.

See Them Building 99

Olov Hartman
Tr. by Caryl and Ruth Micklem

Sven-Erik Bäck
Babel's Tower

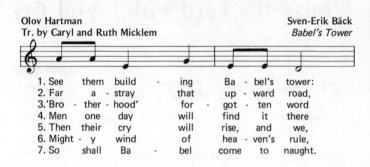

1. See them build - ing Ba - bel's tower:
2. Far a - stray that up - ward road,
3. 'Bro - ther - hood' for - got - ten word
4. Men one day will find it there
5. Then their cry will rise, and we,
6. Might - y wind of hea - ven's rule,
7. So shall Ba - bel come to naught.

1. slaves the stones are carry - ing: here no man
2. man, be - come a stran - ger, goes hun - gry
3. down the grass - y hill - side re - ject - ed
4. and will rec - og - nize it as key - stone
5. each in his own lan - guage shall hear of
6. storm - ing ev - ery bar - rier will blow for -
7. Where it stood shall flou - rish the har - vest

1. cares for bro - ther man: Ky - ri - e - lei - son!
2. at his bro - ther's board: Ky - ri - e - lei - son!
3. from that build - ing lies. Ky - ri - e - lei - son!
4. of God's hill and house. Hal - le - lu - ja!
5. bro - ther - hood once more, Hal - le - lu - ja!
6. ev - er where it wills, Hal - le - lu - ja!
7. of God's bro - ther - hood. Hal - le - lu - ja!

100
Praise the Lord with Joyful Cry

Fred Kaan

Lawrence F. Bartlett
One-fifty
Descant by John Wilson

1. Praise the Lord with joy - ful cry: let the mood of praise run high. Praise Him who with might - y deeds hu - man great - ness far ex - ceeds.

2. Praise Him with the sound that swings, with per - cuss - ion, brass and strings. Let the world at ev - ery chance praise Him with a song and dance.

Descant: Praise _____ the Lord, _____

3. Praise with life _____ and voice the Lord,

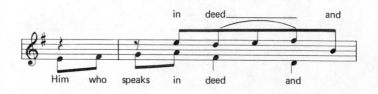

in deed _____ and

Him who speaks in deed and

word, _____ who ____ to life or-

word, Who to life _____ the world or-

dained: our praise _____ un-re-strained! ____

dained: let our praise be un-re-strained!

101

Rejoice with Us in God

F. Pratt Green

Alec Wyton
Routley

Re - joice with us in God the Trin - i - ty, The

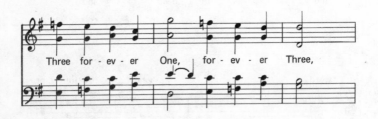

Three for - ev - er One, for - ev - er Three,

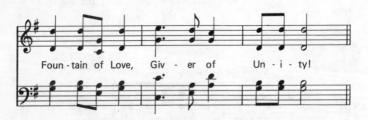

Foun - tain of Love, Giv - er of Un - i - ty!

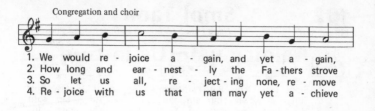

Congregation and choir

1. We would re - joice a - gain, and yet a - gain,
2. How long and ear - nest - ly the Fa - thers strove
3. So let us all, re - ject - ing none, re - move
4. Re - joice with us that man may yet a - chieve

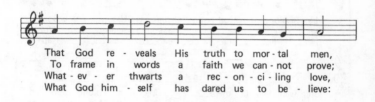

That God re - veals His truth to mor - tal men,
To frame in words a faith we can - not prove;
What - ev - er thwarts a rec - on - ci - ling love,
What God him - self has dared us to be - lieve:

Un - veils for all to see, In what He
But O how dead our creeds Un - less they
All ills that still di - vide The fold of
The man - y live as one, Each lov - ing

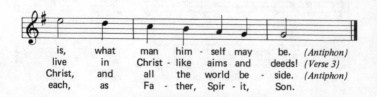

is, what man him - self may be. *(Antiphon)*
live in Christ - like aims and deeds! *(Verse 3)*
Christ, and all the world be - side. *(Antiphon)*
each, as Fa - ther, Spir - it, Son.

102 Smol Taon

(A Pidgin English Christmas Carol)

Ellison Suri

Ellison Suri
Smol Taon

1. Smol taon long Beth-le-hem__ Ji-sas smol be-bi blong__ God bon Kres-mas-de.__ Bon__ long wan-fa-la mere__ Ma-mi blong hem an Jos-eph dad-i tu.__ En-sel se-fad King Ta-lem gud-fa-la nius. Wait-man, blak-man, ev-ri-wan hap-i tu.__ Gud nius hem kam long wol,__ __ Ji-sas Mas-ta blong yiu-mi ev-ri-wan.

2. Suit Ji-sas dip-em slip__ An-tap sofit hei__ in-saet kau-haus long naet. Ol-o raon an ev-ri-wea__ En-sel blong heven sing-em suit mel-o-di.__

3. Tank-iu, tank-iu God__ Yiu kaen tu-mas__ long mi-fa-la ev-ri-wan. Hap-i hap-i Kres-mas de__ Ji-sas Sev-ia blong yiu-mi kam tru nao.__

Thanks to God   103

R. T. Brooks

Peter Cutts
Wylde Green

1. Thanks to God_ whose Word was spo - ken In the
2. Thanks to God_ whose Word in - car - nate Glo - ri -
3. Thanks to God_ whose Word is an - swered By the

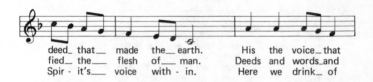

deed_ that_ made the_ earth. His the voice_ that
fied_ the_ flesh of_ man. Deeds and words_and
Spir - it's_ voice with - in. Here we drink_ of

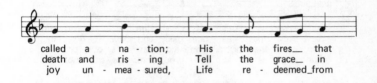

called a na - tion; His the fires_ that
death and ris - ing Tell the grace_ in
joy un - mea - sured, Life re - deemed_from

tried her worth. God has_ spo - ken;_
heav - en's plan. God has_ spo - ken;_
death and sin. God is_ speak - ing;_

Praise_ Him_ for His o - pen Word.

104   The Love of God

Anders Frostenson
Tr. by Fred Kaan

Lars Ake Lundberg
Guds Kärlek

1. The love of God is broad like beach and mead-ow,
2. We long for free-dom where our tru-est be-ing
3. But there are walls that keep us all di-vid-ed;
4. O, judge us, Lord, and in your judg-ment free us,

wide_ as the wind, and an e-ter-nal home.
is___ giv-en hope and cour-age to un-fold.
we___ fence each oth-er in with hate and war.
and_ set our feet in free-dom's o-pen space;

God leaves us free to seek Him or re-ject Him,
We seek in free-dom space and scope for dream-ing,
Fear is the bricks-and-mor-tar of our pris-on,
take us as far as your com-pas-sion wan-ders_

He_ gives us room to an-swer 'yes' or 'no'.
and_ look for ground where trees and plants can grow.
our_ pride of self the pris-on coat we wear.
a-mong the chil-dren of the hu-man race.

The love of God is broad like beach and

mead-ow, wide_ as the wind, and an e-ter-nal home.

They Saw You as the Local Builder's Son

Anders Frostenson
Tr. by Fred Kaan

Verner Ahlberg

1. They saw you as the lo-cal build-er's son, and there-fore out of house of prayer and town they chased you, by your pro-phe-cy en-raged, in-to the dark - ness, to the moun-tain edge.

2. They did not see in you the na-tion's hope, or see you take and drink the bit - ter cup. They did not rec - og - nize the love di-vine in you, who bore a - way our guilt and sin.

3. They did not see your hand in an - guish curled, your hand that heals, the hand that made the world. They failed to see, when dark - ness came at noon, that on your cross your sav - ing work was done.

4. The time will come when ev - ery man shall see your grace is like a stream that fills the sea. You give us of your cov - e - nant the sign, and in your wounds you heal all hu - man pain.

106   The Not-Yet Flower

Based on John 1:1-5

Richard Felciano

the light that shines in dark-ness,

the dark-ness, and the dark-ness knows it not.

5"-8"

mp

LET RING

A member of the community reads aloud.

2 - 5 SECONDS

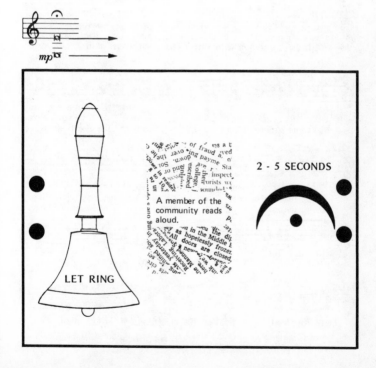

107

Thine Is the Glory

Edmond Louis Budry
Tr. by Richard Hoyle

George Frederick Handel
Maccabeus

1. Thine is the glo - ry, ri - sen__ con - quering Son:
2. Lo, Je - sus meets us, ri - sen__ from the tomb!
3. No more we doubt Thee, glo - rious__ Prince of life;

End - less__ is the vic - tory Thou o'er death hast won.
Lov - ing - ly He greets us, scat - ters fear and gloom.
Life__ is __ nought with - out Thee: aid us in our strife;

An - gels__ in bright rai - ment rolled the stone a - way,
Let __ His __ church with glad - ness hymns of tri - umph sing,
Make __ us __ more than con - querors, through Thy death - less love;

Kept__ the__ fold - ed grave - clothes where the__ bod - y lay.
For__ her__ Lord now liv - eth: death has__ lost its sting.
Bring__ us__ safe through Jor - dan to Thy__ home a - bove.

Thine is the glo - ry, ri - sen,__ con - quering Son:

End - less__ is the vic - tory Thou o'er death hast won.

This Is My Father's World

Maltbie D. Babcock
St. 3 altered by Mary Babcock Crawford*

Malcolm Williamson
Mercer Street

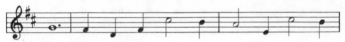

1. This is my Fa - ther's world, And to my lis - tening
2. This is my Fa - ther's world, The birds their car - ols
3. This is our Fa - ther's world, O let us not for -

ears All na - ture sings, and round me rings The
raise, The morn - ing light, the li - ly white, De -
get That though the wrong is great and strong, God

mu - sic of the spheres. This is my Fa - ther's world:
clare their Ma - ker's praise. This is my Fa - ther's world:
is our Fa - ther yet. He trusts us with His world,

I rest me in the thought___ Of rocks___ and trees, of
He shines in all that's fair,___ In the rust - ling grass I
To keep it clean and fair,___ All earth___and trees, all

skies and seas His hand___ the won - ders wrought.
hear Him pass, He speaks to me ev - ery - where.
skies and seas, All crea - tures ev - ery - where.

*Used by permission of Mary Babcock Crawford.

109 This Is the Day

Don and Nancy MacNeill

Daniel Moe
Opening Hymn

1. This is the day, and this the hour of meet - ing, When we can share re - al - i - ty, and all our hopes, be - liev - ing that as we come to - geth - er we are re - made, Re - kind - led now, a liv - ing flame, To light to - mor - row's ways, new light.

2. We share the faith that life is more than liv - ing, Through the long days we come to share this faith in life, be - liev - ing that as we come to - geth - er we find new life, Re - freshed, re - newed, re - stored once more, To find our broth - er here, new life.

3. This is the day, and this the hour of meet - ing, When we pre - pare our - selves to go in - to the world In ser - vice to find you in our broth - er we ded - i - cate Our lives, our - selves to this your world, That it may now be filled with love.

We Do Not Know How to Pray

Adapted by Alan Luff
From R.S.V. *Antiphon*

Erik Routley
Prayer Canticle

We do not know how to pray as we ought____ but the Spir - it Him - self in - ter - cedes for us____ with sighs too deep for words. ____

Verse

1. Ask and it will be given you, and seek and ye shall find, and knock and it will be o - pened to you.____
2. For everyone who asks re - ceives and he who seeks finds and to him who knocks it will be o - pened:____

111

We Know That Christ Is Raised

John B. Geyer

C. V. Stanford
Engelberg

1. We know that Christ is raised and dies no more: Em-braced by fu-tile death He broke its hold: And man's des-pair He turned to blaz-ing joy: Al - le - lu - ia!

2. We share by wa-ter in His sav-ing death: This un-ion brings to be-ing one new cell, A liv-ing and or-ga-nic part of Christ: Al - le - lu - ia!

3. The Fa-ther's splen-dor clothes the Son with life: The Spir-it's fis-sion shakes the Church of God: Bap-tized we live with God the Three in One: Al - le - lu - ia!

4. A new Cre-a-tion comes to life and grows As Christ's new bod-y takes on flesh and blood: The un-i-verse re-stored and whole will sing: Al - le - lu - ia! A - men.

We Meet You, O Christ 112

Fred Kaan

Erik Routley
Durham 72

1. We meet you, O Christ, in man-y a guise; your
(2.) mil-lions a-live, a-way and a-broad; in-
(3.) hear you, O Man, in a-go-ny cry; for
(4.)choose to be made at one with the earth; the

im-age we see in sim-ple and wise. You
volv'd in our life you live down the road. Im-
free-dom you march, in ri-ots you die. Your
dark of the grave pre-pares for your birth. Your

live in a pal-ace, ex-ist in a
pris-on'd in sys-tems you long to be
face in the pa-pers we read and we
death is your ris-ing, cre-a-tive your

shack; we see you, the gar-d'ner, a
free; we see you, Lord Je-sus, still
see. The tree must be plant-ed by
Word; the Tree springs to life and our

1, 2, 3.

tree on your back. 2. In
bear-ing your tree. 3. We
hu-man de-cree. 4. You

4.

hope is re-stored.

113 Weary of All Trumpeting

Martin Franzmann

Hugo Distler
Trumpets
Adapted by Jan Bender

1. Wea - ry of all trum - pet - ing,
2. Cap - tain Christ, O low - ly Lord,
3. To the tri - umph of Your cross

Wea - ry of all kill - ing, Wea - ry of all
Ser - vant King, Your dy - ing Bade us sheathe the
Sum - mon all men liv - ing; Sum - mon us to

songs that sing Prom - ise, non - ful - fill - ing.
fool - ish sword, Bade us cease de - ny - ing.
live by loss, Gain - ing all by giv - ing.

We would raise, O Christ, one song:
Trum - pet with Your Spir - it's breath
Suff'r - ing all, that men may see

We would join in sing - ing That great mu - sic
Through each height and hol - low: In - to Your self -
Tri - umph in sur - ren - der; Leav - ing all, that

pure and strong, Where - with Heav'n is ring - ing.
giv - ing death, Call us all to fol - low.
we may be Part - ners in Your splen - dor.

When the Pious Prayers 114
We Make

David S. Goodall

David S. Goodall
Pious Prayers

1. When the pi - ous prayers we make are a
2. Through the bright per - suad - ing voice of the
3. Beat the dust and nois - y pain of our

wall of pride, lest the faith - ful few a - wake to the
lies we read, in the self - de - ceiv-ing choice of our
town and street; watch Him flinch-ing at the stain of our

world out - side; when a man won't mix with
lust and greed, though the word of man is
hands and feet; hang the heart of God up -

a race which he dis - ap - proves, on - ly
a mesh that our blind-ness proves, we have
on high though He reigns a - bove— and then

God des-cends to make clean the face of the
seen the Word of the Lord made flesh in the
see Him con - quer - ing come to die in the

1,2.
world He loves.

3.

115

When God Almighty

Michael Hewlett

Northumbrian Air
Keel Row
Adapted by John Maynard

1. When God Al-might-y came to be one of us,
2. Splen-dor of Rome and Lo-cal Au-thor-i-ty,
3. Wise men, they called them, earn-est as-trol-o-gers,
4. Sing, all cre-a-tion, made for His pur-pos-es,

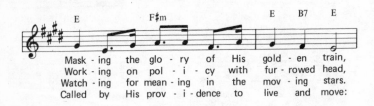

Mask-ing the glo-ry of His gold-en train,
Work-ing on pol-i-cy with fur-rowed head,
Watch-ing for mean-ing in the mov-ing stars.
Called by His prov-i-dence to live and move:

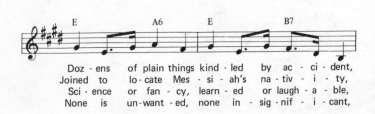

Doz-ens of plain things kind-led by ac-ci-dent,
Joined to lo-cate Mes-si-ah's na-tiv-i-ty,
Sci-ence or fan-cy, learn-ed or laugh-a-ble,
None is un-want-ed, none in-sig-nif-i-cant,

And they will nev-er be the same a-gain.
Just where the pro-phets had al-read-y said.
Theirs was a vi-sion that was brought to pass.
Love needs a u-ni-verse of folk to love.

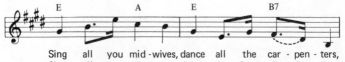

Sing all you mid-wives, dance all the car-pen-ters,
Sing all you tax-men, dance the Com-mis-sion-ers,
Sing all you wise-men, dance all the sci-en-tists,
Old men and maid-ens, young men and child - ren,

Sing all the pub-li-cans and shep-herds too.
Sing civ-il ser-vants and po-lice-men too.
Wheth-er your the-o-ries are false or true.
Black ones and col-ored ones and white ones too.

God in His mer-cy us-es the com-mon-place,
God in His pur-pose us-es the gov-ern-ments,
God us-es know-ledge, God us-es ig-nor-ance,
God on His birth-day, and to e-ter-ni-ty,

God on His birth-day had a need of you.
God on His birth-day had a need of you.
God on His birth-day had a need of you.
God took up-on Him-self the need of you.

116 God of Grace and God of Glory

Harry Emerson Fosdick

Charles Wuorinen
Mannheim

1. God____ of grace____ and God____ of
2. Lo!____ the hosts____ of e - vil
3. Cure ____ Thy chil - dren's war - ring
4. Set____ our feet____ on lof - ty

glo - ry, On Thy peo - ple pour____ Thy
round us Scorn thy Christ, as - sail____ His
mad - ness, Bend our pride to Thy____ con -
pla - ces; Gird our lives that they____ may

pow - er; Crown____ Thine an - cient
ways!____ From____ the fears____ that
trol.____ Shame____ our wan - ton,
.be____ Ar - mored with____ all

church's sto - ry; Bring____ her bud to glo-rious
long have bound us Free____ our hearts to faith and
self - ish glad-ness, Rich____ in things and poor in
Christ-like grac - es In____ the fight to set men

flower. _____ Grant us wis - dom,
praise. _____ Grant us wis - dom,
soul. _____ Grant us wis - dom,
free. _____ Grant us wis - dom,

Grant us____ cour - age____ for the
Grant us____ cour - age____ for the
Grant us____ cour - age____ lest we
Grant us____ cour - age____ that we

fa - cing of this hour.__
liv - ing of these days.__
miss Thy king-dom's goal.__
fail not man nor Thee.__ A - men.

The Glory of Our King 117

Margaret B. Cropper

American Folk Tune
Morning Song

1. The glo - ry of our__ King was__ seen when
2. The glo - ry of our__ King was__ seen when,
3. The glo - ry of our__ King was__ seen on

He came rid - ing by, And__ all the__ chil-dren
with His arms stretched wide To__ show His__ love to
the first Eas - ter day, When__ Christ rose__ up, set

waved and__ sang, Ho - san - na, King__ most high!
ev - ery - one, Je - sus was cru - ci - fied.
free from__ death, to love, to guide,__ to stay.

TOPICAL INDEX

GENERAL INDEX